# OUR LADY'S LITANY

# Our Lady's Litany

## READINGS AND REFLECTIONS

By REV. A. BISKUPEK, S.V.D.

THE BRUCE PUBLISHING COMPANY
MILWAUKEE

IMPRIMI POTEST:

L. MACK, S.V.D.
*Provincialis*

NIHIL OBSTAT:

JOHN A. SCHULIEN, S.T.D.
*Censor librorum*

IMPRIMATUR:

✠ ALBERTUS G. MEYER
*Archiepiscopus Milwauchiensis*

January 11, 1954

(Second Printing — 1955)

*Library of Congress Catalog Card Number: 54–7548*

# Contents

# CONTENTS

# OUR LADY'S LITANY

# 1854-1954

IT WAS on the eighth of December, 1854, that Pius IX, surrounded by an immense gathering of cardinals, bishops, priests, and faithful, solemnly declared: "The doctrine which holds that the Blessed Virgin Mary was preserved from the stain of original sin in the very first moment of her conception through a unique privilege of divine grace in view of the merits of Jesus Christ, Saviour of the human race, is revealed by God and therefore firmly and steadfastly to be believed by all the faithful."

The year 1954 marks the first centenary of this momentous event. In a magnificent encyclical, *Fulgens Corona*, Pope Pius XII solemnly proclaimed the year 1954 as the *Year of Mary* and called upon the faithful to spend it in such a way as to make it a year of grace and heavenly blessings for the renewal of the world in Christ. He writes, "This centenary celebration should not only serve to revive Catholic faith and earnest devotion to the Mother of God in the souls of all, but Christians should also, in as far as possible, conform their lives to the image of the same Virgin . . . our most sweet Mother wishes for nothing more, never rejoices more than when she sees those whom, under the cross of her Son, she has adopted as children in His stead, portray the lineaments and ornaments of her own soul in thought, word, and deed."

A fuller realization of the ideal of life as presented by the immaculate Mother of God will mean a revitalization of Christian energy that has been alarmingly depleted by the soft comforts of our materialistic age. In the midst of the lowering clouds of materialism we need a spiritual outlook on life. Out of it will come hope in apparent hopelessness, courage in the face of mounting evil, the Christian spirit that sees beyond the tribulations of this time the sunshine and peace of the eternal homeland.

The thoughts presented here on the Litany of the Blessed Virgin, also called the Litany of Loreto, are meant to serve this purpose. This is one of the many Marian litanies, or praises of Mary, composed during the Middle Ages. The place of honor it now holds in the life of the Church is due to its faithful use at the shrine of the Holy House at Loreto. It was definitely approved by Sixtus V in 1587, and all other Marian litanies were suppressed, at least for public use. Its forty-nine titles and invocations set before us Mary's exalted privileges, her holiness of life, her amiability and power, her motherly spirit and queenly majesty. The principle that has been followed in their interpretation is the one enunciated by the same Pius IX: "God enriched her so wonderfully from the treasury of His divinity, far beyond all angels and saints with the abundance of all heavenly gifts, that she . . . should show forth such fullness of innocence and holiness, than which a greater under God is unthinkable and which, beside God, no one can even conceive in thought." Hence, whatever virtue and holiness is found in angels and saints must be present in Mary in an immeasurably higher degree.

Reflection on the titles of the litany, therefore, will unfold before us the grand picture of our heavenly Mother, even though we know only little about her life. We will also come to see why Mary's example, guidance, and help is the need of the hour. In fact, the repeated spectacular apparitions of the

Blessed Virgin since the days of La Salette are impressive calls, addressed to mankind and to the faithful in particular, to turn for help to their heavenly Mother. The pleadings of her divine Son in the revelations of the Sacred Heart have not succeeded in bringing the world back to God; will men heed the pleadings of His and their Mother?

# Holy Mary

TO BE holy is the first and foremost task of the Christian. A certain minimum of holiness is necessary for salvation, but the higher degrees of holiness are the aspiration and hope of all true lovers of God. Nothing bestows upon man greater worth and dignity. The beginning of Christian holiness was given us in baptism, and it is the will of God that we guard and develop it. Therefore St. Peter writes, "As the One who called you is holy, be you also holy in all your behavior; for it is written, 'You shall be holy, because I am holy'" (1 Pet. 1:15). As Mary is our leader to Christ, so she is our leader to holiness. The more we appreciate and desire her guidance, the more freely she can act. Hence our first petition in the litany is: Holy Mary, pray for us.

## HOLINESS

When St. Paul tells us that by baptism we have been transformed into Christ, when St. Peter speaks of the Christian as having been made a partaker in the divine nature, when St. John reminds us that we are children of God, all these inspired writers state the same truth: we have been raised to a higher order of life, we have been incorporated into Christ the Holy One, we abide in Him and He in us, we live because of Him as He lives because of the Father. This divine life is the most precious treasure given into our care. In virtue of this life we are holy, but we are to become more holy from day to day, "for this is the will of God, your sanctification" (1 Thess. 4:3).

Mary, the Mother of the Holy One and full of grace, must be holy; the Queen of all saints must possess the highest degree of holiness. This holy Mother is also our Mother, and she desires nothing more than to see her children resemble her and her divine Son. Therefore we turn to her more than to any other saint in our efforts to become holy. In doing this we are encouraged by the beautiful words of Pius XII: "There is no one who has followed in the footsteps of the incarnate Word more closely and with more merit than she; and no one has more power over the Sacred Heart of the Son of God and through Him with the heavenly Father. . . . Since she is, therefore, Mother of mercy, our life, our sweetness, and our hope, let us all cry to her, mourning and weeping in this vale of tears, and confidently place ourselves and all we have under her patronage. . . . She teaches us all virtues; she gives us her Son and with Him all the help we need, for God wishes us to have everything through her" (*Mediator Dei*).

## THE NAME OF MARY

There is no agreement as to the exact meaning of the name of Mary, and many interpretations of it have been given. Among these interpretations the most popular must be said to be: Mistress and Star of the Sea.

As Mother of Christ Mary exercised authority over her divine Son; should she not have been given authority over her spiritual children, the other Christs? Having co-operated with her divine Son in the sacrifice of our salvation, should she not have authority over those toward whose salvation she contributed so much? Let us listen to the way in which holy Church speaks of this authority on the feast of Mary, the Mediatrix of all graces. In the antiphon for the *Magnificat* of the first Vespers she puts these words on the lips of Mary: "Behold, my Lord has delivered all things to me; there is nothing that is not subject to my power, nothing that He did not turn over to me." In the antiphon for the *Benedictus* we hear the words of God conferring this authority upon her: "Without thy authorization no one in the whole land shall move hand or foot." But Mary's authority is kind and gentle, loving and appealing. She is like her divine Son meek and humble of heart; she loves those over whom she rules and uses her authority only to make them happy for time and eternity.

Life is often compared to a journey across a sea agitated by violent storms, with waves rising to frightening heights and falling to abysmal depths. The strong winds of temptations and adversities blow all around us. We feel that we are in danger of losing life and all. Yet we are not left without hope. There is a star in the sky that lights up our way and shows us the right course through the raging waves: Mary, the Star of the sea. This star is ever shining in peaceful radiance, untouched by the fury of the storms, ever pointing to heaven; it speaks to us of eternal peace that awaits us in the heavenly homeland. It remains for us to look up to this star and to follow its guidance; it is the only way to peace and safety. The love-inspired words of St. Bernard will ever remain true: "O you all who are tossed about on the stormy waters of life and exposed to its violent tempests, do not turn away your eyes from this bright star of the sea, if you would not be swallowed up by storm. When tornadolike temptations assail you and your boat is drifting upon rocks, look up to the star, call upon Mary. When buffeted by the billows of pride, of ambition, bitterness, envy, look up to the star, call upon Mary. When anger or avarice or the violence of sensual passions beat upon the boat of your soul, look up to Mary. When feeling crushed by the burden of sin, appalled by the foulness of a guilty conscience, terrified by the thought of the judgment to come, sinking into an abyss of sadness, a whirlpool of despair, then think of Mary, call upon her holy name. Following her you will never go astray, invoking her you will never lose hope, thinking of her you will make no mistake. . . . Thus you will learn by your own experience how truly it is said that the Virgin's name is Mary — Star of the Sea" (Feast of the Most Holy Name of Mary, second nocturn).

# Holy Mother of God

FOUR invocations in the Litany of Loreto refer to Mary's divine motherhood; she is called Mother of God, Mother of Christ, Mother of the Creator, Mother of the Saviour. Upon closer examination these titles open up for us wonderful vistas into the greatness of Mary and the incomprehensible riches of divine wisdom, power, and love manifested in the economy of man's salvation.

The first of these titles states the basic truth: Mary is the Mother of God. Thus it was defined at the Council of Ephesus, in the year 431, against Nestorius, "If anyone does not confess that Emmanuel is God in truth, and therefore the holy Virgin Mother of God, since she brought forth according to the flesh the incarnate Word of God, let him be anathema" (Denz., 113).

There is but one God, that is, one divine nature, but in that one God there are three distinct Persons. In virtue of her divine motherhood Mary must therefore enter a most intimate relationship with each one of these divine Persons.

## SANCTUARY OF THE BLESSED TRINITY

As Mother of God Mary becomes the most sacred sanctuary of the Most Blessed Trinity. The very Godhead, the divine Life and Operations, abides in Mary as long as she carries the incarnate Word of God beneath her heart. In her the Father begets the Son, the Son proceeds from the Father, the Holy Spirit is breathed forth in the eternal love of Father and Son. In her dwell Eternity, Omnipotence, Immensity, and all other divine perfections. In view of all this St. Thomas can say: "Mary, by the fact that she is the Mother of God, possesses a certain infinite dignity, arising out of the infinite good, which is God" (I, 26, 6, 4).

## RELATION TO FATHER

As Mother of God Mary can call Him her Son whom the Father begets from all eternity. The overwhelming majesty of this fact is set in striking relief in the Christmas liturgy of holy Church. In the Introit of the first Mass we listen to the voice of the Father: "The Lord hath said to me: 'Thou art my son; this day I have begotten thee.'" In the Gospel of the same Mass St. Luke records: "And she brought forth her firstborn son, and wrapped him in swaddling clothes, and laid him in a manger." This glorious Mother can say to this her first-born Son, who is the same only-begotten Son of the eternal Father: "Thou art my Son; this day I have given thee birth." The Introit of the third Mass proclaims the joyful news: "A child is born to us and a son is given to us. . . ." Yet this Child is He, of whom St. John says in the Gospel of this Mass: "In the beginning was the Word, and the Word was with God, and the Word was God. . . . And the Word was made flesh and dwelt among us."

Since through Mary the Son of the Father has in all truth become man, He can now honor, obey, worship, offer sacrifice to the Father, which He could not do before because of the equality of nature. Now one act of worship on the part of the divine Son confers upon the Father infinitely more honor and glory than the combined honor and glory rendered Him by all angels and saints. This is a mystery so profound and incomprehensible that all we can do is admire and adore.

RELATION TO SON

Through Mary's motherhood the Son of God becomes the Son of Man, the Head of the human race; it is in Mary that He celebrates His nuptials with the human race for the purpose of begetting spiritual children of God. So says Leo XIII: "The eternal Son of God, about to assume human nature for the redemption and exaltation of man, and for that reason to enter a certain mystical marriage with the whole human race, did not do so until He had received the full consent of the chosen Mother, who in a certain way acted the part of the human race" (*Octobri mense,* 1891).

The fruit of this marriage is the Church. According to Pius XII: "The Church was born from the side of our Saviour on the cross like a new Eve, mother of all living" (*Mystici Corporis*). But, according to the same encyclical, "Mary offered Him on Golgotha to the eternal Father for all the children of Adam, sin-stained by his fall, and her Mother's rights and Mother's love were included in the holocaust." As Mary together with the Holy Spirit built the physical body of Jesus, so she now together with her divine Son builds up His mystical body. The divine life that will quicken the Church is in Christ, but

He will release it only through Mary. Leo XIII thus expresses this thought: "With no less propriety may we say that of the immense treasures which the Lord has produced, by the will of God nothing whatsoever is to be imparted to us except through Mary. As no one can come to the Father except through the Son, so in almost the same manner no one can come to Christ except through Mary" (*Octobri mense*).

Thus it is through Mary that the Word of God, begotten of the Father in the silence of eternity, in inaccessible light, enters this world. Now the Word of God can speak the words of God in the language of men, can place Himself at the head of the human race and lead men in rendering to the Father adoration and worship, such as men could never have rendered otherwise.

RELATION TO HOLY SPIRIT

Mary's relationship to Father and Son finds its completion in her relation to the Holy Spirit. The Holy Spirit proceeds from the Father and the Son; no Person proceeds from Him. Now in the mystery of the Incarnation the Holy Spirit overshadows the Blessed Virgin and makes her the Mother of Christ; the fruit of Mary's chaste womb is also the fruit of His love. And through Jesus and Mary the fruit of His love will also be all the members of the mystical body of Christ, for they are born again to the life of the children of God through water and the Holy Spirit.

Mary is called the Spouse of the Holy Spirit. The very name stands for mutual love, mutual self-surrender — in the case of two human persons, within the limits of the law of God; in the case of a divine and human person, absolute and unconditional on the part of the human person. To no other human person did the Holy Spirit give Himself with such fullness of grace and love; no other person did He associate with

Himself so intimately in the sanctification of souls. On the other hand, from no other human person did He receive such complete, perfect, loving surrender as from Mary.

These relations of the Mother of God to the three divine Persons so wonderfully unite God and men, produce such harmony in the works of God, that Mary has been called the complement of the Blessed Trinity. This expression surely does not imply that she added anything of her own to the perfection of the divine Persons, but it does imply that God decreed from all eternity to unite the whole of creation with Himself in a mysterious union of life and love through the Incarnation of the divine Word, and that in the realization of this decree Mary was to co-operate in a more excellent way than any other creature.

Mother of God — infinite love and condescension on the part of God, infinite exaltation on the part of man — all so sublime, so full of mystery, that it were unbelievable, were it not a dogma of our holy faith: Mary is the Mother of God.


# Holy Virgin of Virgins


THE first Lateran Council states: "If anyone contrary to the teaching of the Fathers does not confess, in the literal and true sense of the words, that the Mother of God, the holy and ever virgin and immaculate Mary . . . conceived of the Holy Spirit without the seed of man, gave birth to Him without the loss of virginity, and remained an inviolate virgin also after birth: let him be anathema" (*Denz.*, 256). The Council of Trent declares: "The same Most Blessed Virgin is the true

Mother of God, ever persevering in her virginity, that is, before, in, and after the birth of Jesus" (*Denz.*, 993). And holy Church in the Preface for the Masses of the Blessed Virgin joyfully proclaims that the Mother of God "sent forth into the world the eternal Light amid the glory of enduring virginity."

The virginal birth of the Messias is the sign given to the house of David by the prophet Isaias: "Therefore the Lord himself shall give you a sign. Behold a virgin shall conceive and bear a Son, and his name shall be called Emmanuel" (Isa. 7:14). Mary, the Virgin of virgins, understood the mind of God as no other virgin ever understood it. We cannot assume that in her humility she aspired after the honor of divine motherhood. But, seeing that God had thus given preference to virginity in the economy of man's salvation, she must have concluded that a virginal life would be the most fitting way of rendering service to God in preparation for the coming of the Messias. The Messias would be the great servant of God — would she not hasten His coming by offering to God her virginal service? The sacrifice of bulls and goats ascended to the throne of God with an odor of sweetness — would He not be pleased with the sacrifice of her virginal life? Emmanuel would be born of a virgin Mother — would He not be pleased to be received by a choir of virgins ready for service? The Holy Spirit who had chosen Mary for His immaculate Spouse had given her this sublime evaluation of virginity.

VIRGINAL MOTHERHOOD

Virginity as part of the total consecration of the Blessed Virgin to the service of God was a prerequisite for divine motherhood. St. Thomas has probably stated the reasons for this as clearly and succinctly as they can be stated. According to this great doctor it was postulated by the following reasons: It was not fitting that the Son of the eternal Father should also have a father on earth; this would be derogatory to the dignity of the divine fatherhood.

It was fitting that the Word of God proceeding from the Father without any impairment of the latter should in His incarnation cause no impairment to His Mother.

The Word of God became man in order to take away the sins of men; it was fitting, therefore, that He should not enter this world in the way in which sin is transmitted.

The purpose of redemption was that men should be born again as children of God — not of the will of the flesh nor of the will of man, but of God. It was fitting, therefore, that a pattern of this rebirth be given at the very beginning of the Redeemer's life.

Virginal fecundity is the one distinction which belongs exclusively to Mary and makes her the Virgin of virgins. St. Bernard has expressed this idea beautifully: "There is nothing that delights me more but at the same time fills me with greater awe than to speak on the glory of the Virgin Mary. If I praise her virginity, many virgins will present themselves who have followed her; if I extol her humility, there will perhaps be found, though few, such as according to the word of our Lord have become meek and humble of heart; if I should desire to magnify the multitude of her mercies, there will be some men and women who also were distinguished by their mercy. There is one thing in which she is seen to be the only one, with no one to precede and no one to follow her — she alone glories in the joys of motherhood together with the honor of virginity" (Octave of the Assumption, former Office).

SPIRITUAL MOTHERHOOD

The very purpose of the Incarnation implies that the Mother of the incarnate Word of God should also become the spiritual

Mother of all men. It follows from the part which Mary had in the sacrifice of our salvation. As Pius XII says: "As another Eve she offered Him on Golgotha to the eternal Father for all the children of Adam sin-stained by his fall, and her mother's rights and mother's love were included in the holocaust. Thus she who corporally was the mother of our Head, through the added title of pain and glory, became spiritually the mother of all His members" (Mystici Corporis).

A mother's office is to give life and then to foster and develop that life. The life of which we speak here is the life of grace, which makes us partakers in the life of God and thus children of God. This divine life vivifying the soul can, in the case of those who have the use of reason, be developed ordinarily only through the influence of actual grace, particularly through the graces of the Blessed Eucharist. The latter, as sacrifice, is the unbloody renewal of the sacrifice of the cross; as Communion, it is the Food of which Jesus says: "He who eats my flesh and drinks my blood has life everlasting . . . abides in me and I in him . . . shall live forever" (Jn. 6:55 ff.). Yet Mary gave us the divine High Priest and Victim, the Bread of life. Mary was most intimately associated with Jesus in His sacrifice and for that reason she became the Mediatrix of all graces; all graces coming down to us pass through her hands. Thus, as we have received the life of grace through Jesus and Mary, so it is sustained, developed, and prepared for its heavenly perfection through Jesus and Mary.

The spiritual motherhood of Mary will be active to the end of time. In the words of Pius XII: "She continued to show for the Mystical Body of Christ . . . the same mother's care and ardent love, with which she clasped the Infant Jesus to her warm and nourishing breast. May she, then, the most holy Mother of all Christ's members . . . never cease to beg from

Him that a continuous, copious flow of graces may pass from its glorious Head into all the members of the Mystical Body" (*Mystici Corporis*).

SIGNIFICANCE FOR CHURCH

The virginal fecundity and spiritual motherhood of the Virgin of virgins is the inspiration of thousands of women who consecrate their lives to God in the religious state. They wish to beget spiritual children for Christ. Their life of total consecration to the Spouse of their souls fulfills eminently the desire for motherhood which God has implanted into the nature of woman. We may add that in like manner total consecration to the highest ideals in the service of God with a view to spiritual fatherhood is the inspiration of the priesthood and the religious brotherhood.

There is no other religious body that has as high a regard for the married state as the Catholic Church; yet the same Church points to a higher ideal in consecrated virginity and spiritual parenthood. The Church needs both, virginal fecundity and spiritual parenthood, in her life-giving mission, and God has given her the ideal and pattern for both in the holy Virgin of virgins.

# Mother of Christ

THE Incarnation reveals the stupendous grandeur of the divine plan in regard to mankind. God not only would create, but He would lift up the whole of creation to Himself, to a participation in His divine life. He Himself would become man and be mankind's Teacher, King, and Priest — the Christ, God's Anointed. And so Mary, "in a marvelous birth . . . brought Him forth as source of all supernatural life and presented Him, new-born, as Prophet, King and Priest to those, who were the first come of Jews and Gentiles to adore Him" (*Mystici Corporis*). As Mother of Christ Mary is not only the foremost beneficiary of the Incarnation but also most intimately associated with her divine Son in the exercise of His prophetic, royal, and priestly office.

## CHRIST

It is a tragic fact of history that man, endowed with a mind to know God and with a will to love Him, should have fallen into those unspeakable abberrations of pagan idolatry, and should follow in our own days the even more degrading errors of atheistic and materialistic philosophy. "While professing to be wise, they have become fools" (Rom. 1:22). It is a fearful illustration of the havoc original sin has wrought in the minds of men and of the influence Satan exercises in the world. Christ, the incarnate Word of God, came to speak to men the words of God and to teach them the ways of truth. He solemnly declares before Pilate: "This is why I was born, and why I have come into the world, to bear witness to the truth" (Jn. 18:37). To make sure that this truth would reach all men, He founds the Church and commissions her to make all men His disciples; and in order to protect His Church against all falsifications of the truth, He bestows upon the head of the Church the gift of infallibility in matters of faith and morals.

Christ is King; His is a spiritual kingdom. It is of this fact that Christ speaks to Pilate, in order to allay his fears of a political uprising: "My kingdom is not of this world. If my kingdom were of this world, my followers would have fought that I might not have been delivered to the Jews. But, as it is, my kingdom is not from here" (Jn. 18:36). The royal command for the spiritual conquest of the world is given when Christ sends out His Apostles to teach all men to observe all things He has taught. Since words teach, but examples draw, He places Himself at the head of His followers and shows the way. He does the will of the Father so as always to please Him; He humbles Himself and becomes obedient to death, even death on a cross. But obedience leads to victory; Christ's death upon the cross is His eternal triumph. It is for this reason that Jesus, although foretelling persecutions and suffering, can inspire all His followers with invincible courage: "In the world you will have affliction. But take courage, I have overcome the world" (Jn. 16:33). And so Christ rules as the King and Center of hearts; no earthly king ever possessed the love and loyalty of his followers as He does.

The most excellent of Christ's offices is the priestly office, and the first and foremost function of the priestly office is the offering of sacrifice, in which our relations to God as our Creator and Last End find their most perfect expression. Isaias speaks of the Messias as a sheep led to slaughter because of our sins, the psalmist sees Him as the priest forever according to the order of Melchisedech, and St. Paul speaks of the eternal priesthood of Christ. Christ accepted His priestly mission in the very first moment of His earthly existence: "Therefore in coming into the world he says, 'Sacrifice and oblation thou wouldst not, but a body thou hast fitted to me. . . . Behold I come — to do thy will, O God' " (Hebr. 10:5 ff.). He actually offered His sacrifice, "on the altar of the cross, offering Himself as a stainless peace-offering in order to accomplish the mystery of man's redemption" (Preface, Feast of Christ the King). He wished to perpetuate this bloody sacrifice in an unbloody manner through the instrumentality of priests in holy Mass: "Do this in remembrance of me. . . . For as often as you shall eat this bread and drink the cup, you proclaim the death of the Lord, until he comes" (1 Cor. 11:24 ff.). Yet the sacrifice of the cross and that of the altar are substantially the same, since "the Victim is one and the same, the same is the offering priest . . . the manner of offering alone being different." This is the definite teaching of the Council of Trent. Thus through the sacrifice of Christ sin is atoned, God's justice satisfied, and the whole of creation returned to God from whom it came forth.

### CHRIST'S MOTHER

The mere fact that Mary is the Mother of Christ makes her inseparable from all blessings which Christ has brought to the world as Teacher, King, and Priest. Destined, however, to be also the spiritual Mother of men, she has taken and is taking an eminent part in the work of Christ.

Mary, too, is teacher. She teaches in ways that can neither be seen nor heard externally, but are perceived by faith and experienced by the heart. She teaches by the sinlessness of her life, by her closeness to God in prayer, thought, and desire, by her absolute conformity to the will of God, by her love of souls, by her sufferings for the salvation of men.

Mary is Queen, Queen of the heavens, Queen of all angels and saints, Queen of the human race. She rules by the grace and authority of her divine Son. "Behold," she says, "my Lord has delivered to me all things; there is nothing that is not within my power, nothing that He has not turned over to me" (Feast of Mary, Mediatrix of All Graces). Therefore she is called the suppliant omnipotence. With queenly authority, then, she calls upon men in her Fatima apparitions to stop offending her divine Son and to do penance.

The Mother of Christ, the divine High Priest, though not vested with the priestly office in the strict sense of the word, nevertheless had a more eminent share in the offering of the sacrifice of our salvation than any other saint, for, the Victim on the cross is her Son, and His sentiments and priestly mind are also hers. Her whole life is part and parcel of this sacrifice and so profound and penetrating are her sufferings that she is the Queen of all martyrs. And so Mary's part in Christ's sacrifice is the call and pattern for our participation, by which we must fill up in our bodies what is as yet wanting to the Passion of Christ. St. Peter speaks of the faithful as a royal, a holy priesthood, called to offer spiritual sacrifices acceptable to God through Jesus Christ. These spiritual sacrifices of the faithful receive their consecration, so to say, through union with the eucharistic sacrifice, which they offer, "not only by the hands of the priest, but also to a certain extent, in union with him" (*Mediator Dei*).

The threefold office of Christ, Teacher, King, and Priest, and the part which the Mother of Christ has in the exercise of these offices, point out the only way in which the world can be saved and peace restored to mankind: return to God. "But man turns properly to God, when he acknowledges His supreme majesty and supreme authority; when he accepts divinely revealed truths with a submissive mind; when he scrupulously obeys divine law, centering in God his every act and aspiration; when he accords, in short, due worship to the one true God" (*Mediator Dei*). This means that Christ must be accepted as Teacher, King, and Priest. May Mary, the Mother of Christ, save the world by leading it to her divine Son.

# Mother of Divine Grace

ALL grace given to men in the present order of things has been merited by Christ, of whose fullness we have all received. Divine motherhood is the greatest of all graces ever bestowed upon a human person. From the very nature of the office assigned to Mary it follows that she must have been the first and foremost beneficiary of the graces merited by Christ. She was preserved from original sin, received the fullness of grace, was made the Mother of Christ, before Christ had merited grace, hence in view of the merits of Christ, and that is a more excellent participation in the merits of Christ than granted to the rest of men. Mary is the Mother of divine grace in the sense that her motherhood is a gift of grace, that she received the highest possible degree of grace, that she co-operated with her divine Son in meriting grace and thus became in all truth the Mother of our spiritual life, the Mother of all living. Theologians give us a multiple division of grace; for our purpose it will be sufficient to consider only habitual and actual grace.

## HABITUAL GRACE

This is the grace which formally sanctifies; it enters the very substance of the soul, elevates it, enlivens it with divine life so that by it we become truly "partakers in the divine nature" as St. Peter says. St. John is thrilled by the same thought when he writes, "Behold what manner of love the Father has bestowed upon us, that we should be called children of God; and such we are" (1 Jn. 3:1). It is a stupendous mystery, this penetration of the natural by the supernatural, of the human by the divine, but it is a blissful fact. It is for a fuller participation in this mystery that holy Church prays at the mixing of the wine and water in holy Mass, "to be partakers of the divine nature of Him, who deigned to assume our human nature."

The Mother of the Author of grace must have been full of grace according to the principle stated by St. Thomas that "God prepares and disposes those whom He has chosen for a special task in such a way as to make them capable of performing that task for which He elected them." Mary could not be made divine in the sense of being equal to God, but she could be elevated to such a sublime participation in that divine life as to become worthy, as far as this is possible for a finite being, to be the Mother of the incarnate Word of God, and equal to the task assigned to her in the economy of our salvation. Similarly Pius IX states in connection with the definition of the dogma of the Immaculate Conception: "God enriched her so wonderfully from the treasury of His divinity, far beyond all angels and saints with the abundance of all heavenly gifts . . . such fullness of innocence and holiness, than which a greater one under God is unthinkable and which, beside God, no one can even conceive in thought."

## ACTUAL GRACE

The exalted position of the Mother of God did not exempt her from dependence on actual grace, but rather accentuated that dependence. Her nature was not essentially different from ours, created and finite, and if her office and holiness raised her above all angels and saints, this was the work of grace. To act in harmony with her sublime office she stood in greater need of grace than we. Grace is the foundation of her holiness; but the higher the structure is, the stronger must be the foundation. Grace is the motive power of her love; but the more excellent the works of love are, the stronger must be the energy that sustains it. Like the rest of men Mary could not perform the least supernatural and meritorious act without the assistance of actual grace. The necessity of grace is universal. There is no exception from the words of Christ, "I am the vine, you are the branches. He who abides in me and I in him, he bears much fruit; for without me you can do nothing" (Jn. 15:5); no exception from the principle stated by the Council of Trent: "As the head into the members, the vine into the branches, so does Jesus Christ Himself impart grace to the just; this grace always precedes, accompanies, and follows their good works, and without this grace their works could in no way be pleasing to God and meritorious."

Actual grace is always given in a degree sufficient to carry out the task assigned to a person by God, and generally in proportion to the degree of holiness, the desire for grace, and co-operation with the graces that have been received. Applying this to the Blessed Virgin we can easily conclude that she must have received an abundance of actual grace far exceeding that granted to angels and saints. Grace has produced wonderful results in the lives of the saints through their faithful co-operation; what must we not expect of the Queen of all saints?

Mary is the Mother of divine grace; all that she is and has is the work of grace. But Mary is the Mother of grace not for herself but for our sake. Just as her divine Son came down for us and our salvation, so she became the Mother of divine grace in order to co-operate with Jesus in making us the children of God through grace. Her eagerness to share with us the riches of grace entrusted to her must be measured by her love of Jesus and her love of souls. Christ loves souls, thirsts for their salvation; He has shed His blood for them, the blood which He received from His holy Mother. It is through His Mother that He wishes to enrich us with the treasures of His grace, to ennoble us with heavenly rank and nobility, to make us sharers in His divine nature, children of divine grace.

> "Mother of grace, O Mary blest,
>   To thee, sweet fount of love, we fly;
>   Shield us through life, and take us hence
> To thy dear bosom when we die."
>       (*Little Office of the Blessed Virgin,*
>       *Compline*)

# Mother Most Pure

JESUS CHRIST is the purest of the pure and, therefore, His Mother must be the Mother most pure by the law of divine proportion. Since we speak here of the mother titles of the Blessed One among women, we must refer this title to the ideal of pure motherhood presented to us in the Mother of Jesus. This and the following three titles are therefore of the utmost practical importance for our times, in which "a great number of men, forgetful of that divine work of redemption, either entirely ignore or shamelessly deny the great sanctity of Christian wedlock or even, relying on the principles of a new and utterly perverse morality, too often trample it under foot" (Encyclical on Christian Marriage). Speaking of the most pure Mother in a general way we naturally think of her sinlessness and her ideal attitude toward Motherhood.

## PURITY

Holy Church in the Mass for the Purest Heart of Mary applies to her these words from the Book of Wisdom: "No defiled thing cometh into her. She is the brightness of eternal light and the spotless mirror of God's majesty and the image of his goodness" (Wisd. 7:25). Mary was preserved not only from original sin, but even from the least fault and imperfection. This is the doctrine of the Church as stated by the Council of Trent: "If anyone shall say that a person once justified . . . can for the rest of his life avoid all sins, even the least, unless by a special privilege of God, such as the Church holds concerning the Blessed Virgin, let him be anathema" (*Denz.*, 833). Long before the Council of Trent, St. Ephrem had expressed the faith of the Church in these beautiful words: "Thou alone, O Lord, and Thy Mother, Thou alone are perfectly holy; for in Thee, O Lord, there is no stain, nor is there any blemish in Thy Mother." Absence of sin is the negative element in holiness; there must be added the positive element of virtue and progress. Though full of grace at all times, the Blessed Virgin could and did grow in holiness through her faithful co-operation with grace. The light and splendor of her holy life were like the sun hastening to his noonday brightness. Where there is no darkness there is light, but light can increase in intensity; where there is no sickness there is health, but health can increase in vigor and vitality. Such was the progress of the Blessed Mother of God that from day to day and from hour to hour she reflected more brightly the brightness of eternal light and expressed more definitely and distinctly the image of His goodness.

## Pure Motherhood

Pure motherhood reveals itself in the attitude toward marriage and motherhood. The primary purpose of marriage is the propagation of the human race. "How great a boon of God this is and what a blessing of matrimony is clear from a consideration of man's dignity and his sublime end . . . that they may be worshippers of God . . . not any kind of worshippers of the true God, but children, who are to become members of the Church of Christ, fellow citizens of the saints, and members of God's household . . ." (Christian Marriage). Deliberately and lovingly to aim at this purpose of marriage is pure motherhood.

To speed the coming of the Saviour, who would make men worshipers of God in spirit and in truth, Mary made the vow of virginity as a young girl. Learning that she was chosen to be the virgin Mother of the Messias she consecrated herself to God anew in virginal surrender, proclaiming herself the handmaid of the Lord. The words which the prophet put on the lips of the Messias entering the world were in her heart even though not spoken audibly: "Sacrifice and oblation thou wouldst not, but a body thou hast fitted to me. . . . Behold, I come to do thy will, O God" (Hebr. 9:55). As she finally sees herself Mother of the Saviour, she beholds in Jesus not only her Son, but the Saviour of the world. He belongs to His Father and must do the Father's work. Mary accepts the will of God and, in total surrender of all her claims, she offers Jesus to the Father; this her surrender finds its consummation beneath the cross on Calvary.

## CHRISTIAN MOTHERHOOD

The mission of Christ is continued through the Church. To co-operate with Christ and the Church in accomplishing this mission is the purpose of marriage and therefore it calls for generous, selfless love of God and souls. Children are to be born and raised, not primarily for a worldly career, not for the parents' personal satisfaction and advantage, but for God. That children may know and love God and in all things do His holy will is the object of education. It is in view of this end of marriage that St. Paul can write, "This is a great mystery — I mean in reference to Christ and to the Church" (Eph. 5:32). And God will call some of the children to co-operate with Christ and the Church in the salvation of the world. Parents betray their sacred trust, if in selfish narrow-minded love they obstruct the will of God calling their child to His exclusive service, particularly in the religious or priestly state. Pure Christian motherhood will rejoice and be grateful for such a call and gladly offer the child to the Lord; it is a sublime honor and privilege, which God bestows upon them through such a vocation. There would be more priests and religious to do the work of Christ and the Church if there were more mothers animated by the ideal of pure, Christian motherhood.

This title, Mother most pure, is of eminent practical significance for our times, infected with selfishness and materialism. It points to the place motherhood holds in the plan of Divine Providence, and that is to co-operate with God in the salvation of the world and fill up the number of the elect. O Mother most pure, pray for our Christian mothers.

# Mother Most Chaste

STEEPED in materialism our age has seen a nauseating, frightening glorification of the vice of impurity. The purpose and sanctity of marriage has been lost sight of. "A great number of men, forgetful of that divine work of redemption, either entirely ignore or shamelessly deny the great sanctity of Christian wedlock, or, relying on the principles of a new and utterly perverse morality, too often trample it under foot" (Christian Marriage). The threat of divine punishment hangs over the world as it did before the Deluge, when God decreed to destroy the human race because men had become flesh. So much the more do we need the inspiring ideal of chastity presented to us in the Mother most chaste.

## CHASTITY

Chastity is included in the concept of purity as a part in the whole. As a special virtue it denotes the subjection and control of the sexual appetite according to the dictates of reason and faith in the particular state of life in which a person is placed. We speak of conjugal, celibate, virginal chastity. On the subject of conjugal chastity Pius XI has this to say: "That mutual familiar intercourse between the spouses themselves, if the blessing of conjugal faith is to shine with becoming splendor, must be distinguished by chastity in such a wise that husband and wife must bear themselves in all things according to the law of God and nature, and endeavor always to follow the will of their most wise and holy Creator with the greatest reverence toward the work of God" (Christian Marriage).

Mary, the virgin Mother of Christ, observed in the married state the most perfect virginal chastity. This is not meant for all; it is her exclusive privilege for reasons which we considered in the chapter on the title "Virgin of Virgins." But Mary's virginal life and motherhood emphasize the consecration of the human body to God as the first and foremost element in conjugal chastity. Where this is understood, conjugal chastity has found its strongest support.

## SACREDNESS OF HUMAN BODY

It is through bodily union of the sexes that the human race is propagated — God creating in each case the human soul. "Thus among the blessings of marriage the child holds the first place and, indeed, the Creator of the human race Himself, who in His goodness wished to use men as His helpers in the propagation of life, taught this when, instituting marriage in Paradise, He said to our first parents, and through them to all future spouses, 'Increase and multiply and fill the earth'" (Christian Marriage). Destination to so sacred a purpose reveals the sacredness of man, not only as to soul, but also as to his body. Indeed, the human body is sacred, fashioned according to the laws which God laid upon human nature, quickened by a soul which the divine Spirit breathed into it. The whole man, soul and body, is destined to become a temple of God, member of the mystical body of Christ, and to live eternally in heavenly joy. Does not this idea of the dignity and destiny of man and, consequently, the sacredness of co-operation with the almighty God in giving existence to new human beings also show the intrinsic malice and hideousness of abusing the body in immoral and lustful mingling of the sexes? The great Apostle impresses this idea forcibly upon the Corinthians when he writes: "Do you not know that your bodies are members of Christ: Shall I then take the members of Christ and make them members of a harlot? . . . Or, do you not know that your members are the temple of the Holy Spirit, who is in you, whom you have received from God and that you are not your own?" (1 Cor. 6:15.) The abuse of the body for the gratification of lust poisons the very fountains of life. Once this poison has been injected into a nation and is not stopped in its spread, that nation is on the way to extinction, for, "If anyone destroys the temple of God, him will God destroy; for holy is the temple of God, and this temple you are" (1 Cor. 3:17). And again, "The nation and kingdom that will not serve Thee shall perish, and the Gentiles shall be wasted with desolation" (Feast of Christ the King).

## True to Consecration

Marriage consecrates the human body to God in the most important function of which it is capable. This consecration to be effective and permanent must be based, according to Pius XI, on love — love of God, love of the spouse, love of offspring. Abuse of the generative faculty is a criminal injury inflicted upon the partner under the mask of love. Thus a life of conjugal chastity is in an eminent sense a life of love. In view of human weakness such a life is impossible unless lived in close union with God. Mary, the Mother most chaste, though free from evil concupiscence and all inordinate inclinations, nevertheless practices all those things which insure victory over all evil lusts and temptations. She is given to prayer; God fills her mind and heart. She is always occupied doing the work God has assigned to her; idleness invites the tempter. There is reserve in her contacts with people excluding idle conversations; her eyes and ears are closed to whatever might contaminate the soul. Above all, her heart is all aflame with the love of God, and where God is loved with the whole heart, unlawful love of creatures becomes an impossibility. In like manner the remembrance of God must sanctify the home and keep out of it the spirit of the world, strength must be sought in the frequent reception of the sacraments, the occasions of sin must be avoided. A chaste married life is the fruit of loving consecration of the body with all its faculties and functions to the sublime purpose of marriage, that is, consecration of the married in their whole person to God, their Creator and Last End. Let Mary, the Mother most chaste, be their inspiration and exemplar.

# Mother Inviolate

THAT Mary was an inviolate virgin before, in, and after the birth of Christ is doctrine of the faith. We find in Mary's virginal motherhood cause for admiration, joy, and thanksgiving, but we also know that it is her exclusive privilege, granted her because of the unique place which she occupies in the economy of our salvation; it is not meant for ordinary mothers. However, the loss of virginal integrity through God-willed motherhood cannot be called a violation, but violation is its loss through sinful abuse of the body. Pius XI in his encyclical on Christian Marriage points out the principal violations in this regard; they are adultery, prevention of conception, and abortion. Living up to the ideal of Christian marriage the married can truly imitate the inviolateness of the Blessed Mother and share in the glory of her inviolate motherhood.

## ADULTERY

Adultery is a tearing apart of what God has joined together, not indeed of the marriage bond, which is indissoluble in the sacramental consummated marriage, but of that oneness of mind and mutual trust, usually also of that community of life, which is necessary for the attainment of the ends of marriage; it is a violation of the body and of that sacred mystery which links the married to Christ and the Church. The world rebels against this Christian view of adultery, but "such unworthy and idle opinions are condemned by that noble instinct which is found in every chaste husband and wife, and that even by the light of the testimony of nature alone, a testimony that is sanctioned and confirmed by the command of God, 'Thou shalt not commit adultery,' and the words of Christ, 'Whosoever shall look on a woman to lust after her hath already committed adultery with her in his heart'. The force of this divine precept can never be weakened by a merely human custom, bad example, or pretext of human progress, for just as it is the one and the same 'Jesus Christ, yesterday, and today, and the same forever,' so it is the same doctrine of Christ that abides and of which not one jot or tittle shall pass away till all are fulfilled" (Christian Marriage).

## PREVENTION OF CONCEPTION

The special malice of this violation of the body lies in the fact that the body is used for the gratification of lust while the primary purpose of marriage is frustrated. It is a perversion of the right order, a desecration of marriage, a degrading violation of the body. "The Catholic Church, to whom God has entrusted the defense and the integrity and purity of morals . . . in order that she may preserve the chastity of the nuptial union from being defiled by this foul stain, raises her voice in token of divine ambassadorship and through Our mouth proclaims anew: Any use whatever of matrimony, exercised in such a way that the act is deliberately frustrated in its natural power to generate life, is an offense against the law of God and of nature and those who indulge in it are branded with the guilt of grave sin" (Christian Marriage).

## ABORTION

This is the most grievous and hateful abuse and violation of the maternal body. What else is it but murder, in many cases added to adultery! We shudder at the infernal malice of such an act. It is not only the destruction of bodily life, but also the robbing of the child of the possibility of baptism. The maternal body is changed into an execution chamber, where an innocent, helpless being, the fruit of the womb, is slaughtered. Here again Pius XI speaks in the name of Christ when he denounces this abominable crime: "But another very grave crime is to be noted, which regards the taking of the life of the offspring in the mother's womb. . . . However much we may pity the mother, whose health and even life is gravely imperiled in the performance of the duty allotted to her by nature, nevertheless, what could ever be a sufficient reason for excusing in any way the direct murder of the innocent? This is precisely what we are dealing with here. . . . What is asserted in favor of eugenic and social indication . . . is unthinkable and contrary to the divine precept promulgated in the words of the Apostle, 'Evil is not to be done that good may come of it' (Rom. 3:8). . . . And if the public magistrates not only do not defend them (the offspring), but by their laws and ordinances betray them to death at the hand of doctors and others, let them remember that God is the judge and avenger of innocent blood, which cries from earth to heaven" (Christian Marriage).

Violation of motherhood through the sins mentioned by Pius XI is undoubtedly one of the principal factors in the moral corruption of the world at the present time. It must be the prayer of all Catholics, but especially of all pastors of souls and of the married themselves, that devotion to Mary, the Mother inviolate, may increase and that, through the intercession of the Mother of Christ, Christian mothers may come to realize the sublimity and sacredness of motherhood. Inviolate motherhood may bring to the mother innumerable sorrows and hardships, but the all-powerful grace of God will always be at hand to fortify her. And the day will come when her sorrow shall be changed into joy. The words which the priest addresses to the mother in the blessing after childbirth may well be looked upon as an anticipation of the welcome which will be extended to her by the Lord: "Enter the temple of God, adore the Son of the Blessed Virgin, who has given you your child." Of such a mother it will be true forever: "This woman shall receive a blessing from the Lord and mercy from God her Saviour, for she belongs to the generation of those who seek the Lord" (blessing after childbirth).

# Mother Undefiled

WE CONSIDERED the inviolateness of our Blessed Mother in contrast to the vices prevalent in our days, by which the body is violated and defiled. Such violation of the body is practically always preceded by defilement of the soul: lustful thoughts and desires tarnishing conjugal fidelity, indifference and coldness taking the place of love, the spirit of independence refusing to obey, sloth or love of pleasure crowding out the love and care of offspring. Precisely these things are mentioned by Pius XI as defilements of motherhood in the encyclical on Christian marriage. Mary is the Mother undefiled in her relation to St. Joseph, her husband, and in relation to her divine Child.

RELATION TO HUSBAND

The wife's relation to her husband is according to Pius XI characterized by fidelity, love, and obedience. Conjugal fidelity implies that it is exclusive of any other person; it can exist only between husband and wife. As they become one in the flesh, so they must be first of all one in mind: "By matrimony the souls of the contracting parties are joined and knit together more intimately than their bodies, and that not by any passing affection of sense or spirit, but by a deliberate and firm act of the will; and from this union of souls by God's decree, a sacred and inviolable bond arises. . . . Wherefore conjugal faith or honor demands in the first place the complete unity of matrimony, which the Creator Himself laid down in the beginning when He wished it to be not otherwise than between one man and one woman" (Christian Marriage). Mary, the Mother undefiled, is also the Virgin of virgins; it would be blasphemy to assume even the possibility of unfaithfulness in her.

As to conjugal love the same Pope Pius has this to say: "This conjugal faith blooms more freely, the more beautifully and more nobly, when it is rooted in that more excellent soil, the love of husband and wife. . . . The love, then, of which we are speaking is not based on the passing lust of the moment, nor does it consist in passing words only, but in the deep attachment of the heart which is expressed in action. . . . This outward expression of love in the home demands not only mutual help but must go much further, indeed must have for its primary purpose that man and wife help each other day by day in forming and perfecting themselves in the interior life; so that through their partnership in life they may advance ever more in virtue, and above all that they may grow in true love of God and neighbor, on which dependeth the whole law and the prophets" (Christian Marriage). How Mary must have loved St. Joseph as she watched him in his humble faith and devotion to duty, his patience in trials and ready obedience to the call of God. And with this love there passed over into Joseph's heart more and more of her own love of God, her purity and patience and all the other virtues. Mary and Joseph were truly, in the most noble sense of the word, one heart and one soul.

Conjugal obedience is thus described in the same encyclical on Christian marriage: "Domestic society being confirmed therefore by this bond of love, it is necessary that there should flourish in it 'order of love,' as St. Augustine calls it. This order includes both primacy of the husband with regard to the wife and children, and the ready subjection of the wife and her willing obedience. . . . It forbids that in this body, which is the family, the heart be separated from the head to the great detriment of the whole body and the proximate danger of ruin. For if the man is the head, the woman is the heart, and as he occupies the chief place in ruling, so she may and ought to claim for herself the chief place of love." The Gospel represents St. Joseph as the head of the Holy Family and Mary as subject to him. How could it be otherwise, since she sees in Joseph the representative of the heavenly Father, and her only desire is to be His humble handmaid?

If our times abound with domestic disorder, divorce, and broken homes, is not the underlying reason the lack of faith,

love, obedience, and interest in each other's spiritual welfare?
We need the inspiration and help of the Mother undefiled.

RELATION TO OFFSPRING

The voice of God and nature speaks in Canon 1113: "The
parents are bound by a most serious obligation to provide to the
best of their ability for the religious and moral as well as the
physical and secular education of their children, and to care
for their temporal welfare." Mary is the Mother undefiled in
relation to her divine Son. Jesus grew up under Mary's motherly
care. He is the object of all her attention and love, the more so,
as she knew that she was raising the Lamb of God for the great
sacrifice of our salvation. The ideal attitude of the Christian
mother in the care for her child must always be to prepare it
for the task which Providence will assign to it.

More important than the physical care of the child is its
spiritual training. It seems paradoxical to speak of the spiritual
training of the divine Child. Yet it is in perfect harmony with
the whole economy of the Incarnation. As the Son of God
made Himself dependent upon Mary in His physical life, so
He did in the manifestation of His mental and spiritual life.
Although possessing all the treasures of wisdom and knowledge,
He wished to hide them and to manifest them only to the
extent of His training and experience.

So we must picture to ourselves the Blessed Mother instruct-
ing her divine Child. She teaches Him the prayers which all
the Jewish children would learn at that age, the external forms
observed at prayer and religious services in the synagogue and
Temple. She would speak to Him of the wonderful history of
the people, of the prophets and their prophecies concerning the
coming Messias. These must have been sweet and sacred hours,
when she thus spoke to the divine Child, and from the heart

of Jesus radiated into her heart light and love from on high, forming her heart ever more after His own.

The Christian mother will fulfill her sublimest task in teaching her child the knowledge and love of God. Speaking to her child of the Child Jesus, of Mary and the saints, of guardian angels and the happiness of a pious life, she will see the image of the Christ Child reflected ever more clearly in her offspring. As Jesus, so also her child will advance in wisdom and grace before God and men. And as St. John Chrysostom says, "What is greater than to direct minds, to form the lives of the young? I consider one, who knows how to form the minds of the young, as undoubtedly far surpassing in excellence any painter, or sculptor, or other artist" (Feast of St. Joseph Calasance, homily).

As the tree is bent when it is young so it will grow, as the child is trained so it will develop, and the child of today is the man and woman of tomorrow. A motherhood pure and undefiled will contribute more than anything else to make this world a place of order, peace, and happiness. That this ideal may become a reality is the object of the petition addressed to the Mother undefiled.

# Mother Amiable

AMIABLE is what deserves our love. God is infinitely amiable because He possesses in an infinite degree whatever is lovable. Created beings are amiable to the extent to which they partake in the perfection of God. Next to God the Mother of God is most amiable, because she is the most perfect of all created beings; God Himself loves her above all His creation. Of all the reasons which make Mary the Mother amiable we will consider only one: her beauty. The conclusion that will suggest itself is that we must make ourselves her lovable children by loving and imitating her.

## BEAUTY

According to St. Thomas beauty is whatever pleases by its very sight or perception. God is the Author and Prototype of all beauty, Beauty Itself. He has made the world so beautiful with its starry sky, its enchanting landscapes, lovely mountains and valleys, rivers and lakes, its flowers and birds. Surely He must have made her beautiful who was to be the Queen of all creation.

If types of the Blessed Virgin in the Old Testament were celebrated because of their beauty, what must we not expect of the antitype, of Mary, who was to impress the likeness of her features upon the Son of the eternal Father. Judith, who slew Holofernes, the leader of her people's enemies, "appeared to all men's eyes incomparably lovely" (Judith 10:4). Should she who crushed the head of the hellish serpent and brought liberty to all nations be less beautiful? Of Queen Esther we read that, "she was exceeding fair and her incredible beauty made her appear agreeable and amiable in the eyes of all" (Esth. 2:15). By her beauty she appeased the king and saved her people from destruction. Should Mary, with whom the King of kings was so enamored as to choose her for His Mother and Queen of His kingdom, be less beautiful? The spouse in the Canticle is spoken of as the fairest among women: "How beautiful art thou, my love, how beautiful art thou. . . . Thou art all fair, O my love, and there is not a spot in thee" (Cant. 1:6–9; 4:1, 7). St. Andrew of Crete says that Mary was, as it were, a statue sculptured by God, an exquisitely wrought image of the divine Archetype. St. Bernadette would not look at a picture of the Blessed Virgin after having seen her in vision; the difference would be too distressing. The children of Fatima speak only of the beautiful Lady and all attempts of artists to produce an image of her remain disappointing.

Physical beauty is surpassed by the beauty of the soul, the beauty of innocence, virtue, and holiness. Where it is absent, where sin has left its trace upon the human face, we cannot speak of real beauty any more; there may be a bewitching make-up, the trappings of sensuality, but something will be missing: the reflection of the Beauty ever ancient, ever new. Spiritual beauty is a participation in the beauty of God. It is for this reason that saints tell us, if we could see a soul in the state of sanctifying grace, we would die with delight. This divine beauty also shines through man's mortal frame and explains why saints are so attractive, even though they may be of homely features. Yet among all angels and saints there is none that can compare in grace and holiness with the Blessed Mother of God. So holy Church can ask the wondering question in the Office of the Assumption: "Who is she coming up like the morning dawn, beautiful as the moon, chosen as the sun, terrible like an army in battle formation?"

## OUR DUTY OF LOVE

Love of God is the great commandment of the law. God must be loved above all created things because of His infinite perfection. Catholic teaching is that the more a person possesses of the perfection of God, the more that person deserves our love. So the simple conclusion drawn by theologians is that the angels and saints of God in heaven must be loved most next to God, more even than those who are closest to us in life. Yet, among all angels and saints there is none so close to God, possessing so much of His perfection, as the Blessed Mother of God; therefore it is our duty to love her, next to God, above any and every created being.

We are children of Mary; we ought to be the loving and lovable children of the Mother amiable. We prove our love of Mary by frequent loving thoughts of her. Her wonderful virtues are an inexhaustible source of light and inspiration for a holy life. Loving thoughts are followed by loving desires and deeds. We can daily recite the rosary, the litany, short ejaculations; we can celebrate her feasts with childlike joy, and there will be found innumerable other ways of honoring her, for love is inventive. Such love will lead to the imitation of her virtues, and these virtues will produce in us more and more the likeness of our heavenly Mother and make us pleasing in the sight of God. The likeness of Mary is the likeness of her divine Son, and likeness with Jesus is the sign of predestination, "For those whom he has foreknown, he has also predestined to become conformed to the image of his Son" (Rom. 8:29). For those, who do not love Mary, there is no place in heaven; they do not fit into the heavenly company, for in heaven all love Mary. The Father loves her as His most faithful daughter, the Son loves her as His Virgin Mother and faithful companion in the labors and sufferings of His life, the Holy Spirit loves her as His immaculate Spouse, and all the angels and saints love her as their most glorious Queen and Mother.

Mother amiable, I love thee — increase my love for thee.


# Mother Admirable


IN THOSE whom we love we rejoice to see whatever is good and excellent, whatever distinguishes and raises them above the common. Mary, the Mother amiable, loved more than any earthly mother ever was loved, presents to our affectionate gaze excellencies so great and exalted, that they cannot but add to our love profoundest admiration, speechless awe, and exultant jubilation. She is the Mother admirable because her motherhood is divine and priestly, universal and ever active.

## DIVINE MOTHERHOOD

Even natural motherhood is something mysterious, something divine. God works in the mother. He forms the body of the child, not out of the slime of the earth, but out of the flesh and blood of the mother; not directly and immediately, but by the laws which He has laid down in human nature; then He Himself directly and immediately creates the soul and makes the fruit of the mother's womb a human person. Every mother must agree with the pious and valiant mother of the Machabees as she addressed her youngest son, "I know not how your were formed in my womb; for I neither gave you breath, nor soul, nor life, neither did I form the limbs of every one of you. But the Creator of the world, that formed the nativity of man and that found out the origin of all" (Mach. 7:22).

In Mary the mystery of motherhood is infinitely more profound. She becomes Mother without the co-operation of a father. Her motherhood calls for the direct operation of divine power not only as to the soul but also as to the body of her offspring. In a much more comprehensive sense than any human mother is she the Mother of Jesus. All that is in Christ's body has taken its origin from her; and He, who is born of her, is not only man but also God, the incarnate Word divine. "Admirable" is His name, admirable is His Mother.

## PRIESTLY MOTHERHOOD

The son of an ordinary human mother may become a priest, but the mother's participation in the holy sacrifice offered by her son does not go beyond the participation in the sacrifice that is common to all the faithful. The ordinary human priest offers the divine Victim, not his own body and blood; consequently there is nothing of the mother that enters the sacrifice offered by her son. In the sacrifice offered by our Saviour upon the cross the body nailed to the cross, the blood shed in Christ's Passion is also her flesh and blood; the victim is in the fullest sense of the word her Son, and she offers Him with all her love and all her maternal rights. She is a priestly Mother; her motherhood a priestly, sacrificial motherhood.

## Universal Motherhood

Ordinary motherhood extends to only a limited number of children. In their regard the mother is the proximate cause of their physical life, and she takes care of their education until they have reached maturity; at all events, any direct influence upon the child comes to an end when she dies. Mary's motherhood reaches as far as Christ's redeeming sacrifice. Since Christ died for all, Mary is the Mother of all and her motherhood is active so long as life lasts. "However, Mary is not Mother of the faithful and of infidels, of the just and sinners in exactly the same way. . . . Mary is Mother of infidels in that she is destined to engender them to grace, and in that she obtains for them actual grace, which disposes them for the faith and for justification. She is the Mother of the faithful who are in the state of mortal sin in that she watches over them by obtaining for them the graces necessary for acts of faith and hope, and for disposing themselves for justification. Of those who have died in the state of mortal sin she is no longer the Mother; she *was* their Mother. She is fully the Mother of the just, since they have received sanctifying grace and charity through her. She cares for them with tender solicitude, so that they may continue in grace and grow in charity. She is in an eminent way the

Mother of the blessed, who no longer can lose the life of grace" (Garrigou-Lagrange, *The Mother of the Saviour*). Thus, next to Christ as the principal cause, Mary is active as the secondary cause in giving to the soul the life of grace. Then she continues to be active in her spiritual children's behalf, not only through the years of their physical childhood, but throughout life. Spiritually we remain children, in need of her motherly care, as long as we live.

Hence the axioms: "There is no salvation without Mary," and "No one will be lost who has a tender devotion to Mary," rest on solid foundation. All this also explains why in our days, when the salvation of the faithful is exposed to greater dangers than ever before, Mary shows such a striking solicitude in behalf of the world, and why the Church with ever increasing trust and love turns to her for protection and safety. This is the meaning of the words of Pius XII in consecrating the world to the Immaculate Heart of Mary: "In this tragic hour of human history we confide, entrust, and consecrate to thy Immaculate Heart the holy Church, the mystical body of thy Son Jesus, which bleeds now from so many wounds and is so sorely tried. We consecrate likewise to thy Immaculate Heart the whole world, torn as it is by deadly strife, afire with hatred and paying the penalty of its own wickedness."

There is no end to the discoveries we shall make in contemplating the wonders of Mary's motherhood. Admiration will then pass over into veneration, veneration into imitation, imitation into love and trustful surrender of ourselves to her motherly care.

# Mother of Good Counsel

FOR many centuries our Blessed Mother has been honored under the title of Mother of good counsel. Shortly before the capture of Scutari in Albania by the Turks in 1467, a miraculous picture of this title, the author and age of which is unknown, is said to have been brought by angels from this city to Gennazano in Italy, where it is venerated in the church of the Augustinian Fathers and attracts many thousands of pilgrims every year. In 1903 Leo XIII approved a feast and a special Mass in honor of the Mother of good counsel, which is celebrated in many places on April 26. The confusion of ideas in the world, especially in religious matters, and the widespread social and political turmoil surely emphasize the need of good counsel, which would show men the way out of the chaos of their making and lead them on the way of peace and salvation. The Mother of good counsel, filled with divine counsel, offers help to her helpless children.

## DIVINE COUNSEL

The prophet Isaias speaks of the Messias as the Angel of the great counsel, that is, the messenger of God, sent to carry out the decree of man's redemption. Mary, the Mother of the Angel of the great counsel, must be expected to have a profounder knowledge than any other created mind of the reasons why the Passion and death of the Saviour was chosen as the means to redeem mankind. Pride had to be atoned by humiliation, disobedience by obedience unto death, sinful pleasure by suffering; thus men would come to realize more thoroughly the purpose of their existence, do penance for their sins, and strive after holiness of life.

The life of Mary shows that she fully understood this divine counsel. At the Annunciation she has but one question to ask: How shall this be done? She sees in the poverty of Bethlehem and in the flight to Egypt the divine counsel and she joyfully conforms to it without complaining. She does not waver in her total dedication to the Lord when told by Simeon that a sword of sorrows will pierce her heart, and she perseveres in this attitude of mind and will until all is consummated on Calvary. Thus understanding the divine counsel and having lived according to it, she is qualified to counteract the work of Eve, who listened to the evil spirit and by her counsel to Adam brought ruin and death to the whole human race.

MOTHERLY COUNSEL

So perfectly is Mary of the mind of the Angel of the great counsel that holy Church identifies her counsel with that of divine Wisdom. Against the background of her life, fully conformed to the divine counsel, we feel the truth and motherly concern of Mary, that speaks from the Epistle and Gradual of the feast of the Mother of good counsel; she speaks to us in the words of divine Wisdom inviting us to accept her counsel.

"As the vine I have brought forth a pleasant odor, and my flowers are the fruit of honor and riches." Holy Scripture speaks of the sweet odor of prayer, of sacrifice, of a holy life, because it is pleasing to God, stimulating and inspiring for those who observe it. A holy life is man's greatest honor, because it makes him like unto God and earns for him riches exceeding in value all the wealth of the earth, imperishable, everlasting.

"I am the Mother of fair love, and of fear, and of knowledge, and of holy hope." Fair love engenders holy fear; how could a true lover of God ever offend Him or refuse to fulfill His wishes? Mary is filled with the gift of the fear of the Lord. The fear and love of God impart true knowledge of the meaning of life, protect against the deceptions of the world, and arouse holy hope for the things that God has prepared for those who love Him.

"In me is all grace of the way and of the truth, in me all hope of life and of virtue." Jesus speaks of Himself as the Way, the Truth, and the Life. God is our last end and we must know the way to Him; we know the way by believing the truth of His words and example; we follow the way by living a life of virtue, which will pass over into the life of glory in the blissful vision of God in life eternal. For doing all this we need grace and all grace comes to us through Mary, and thus through Mary we hope to reach our goal.

"Come over to me, all ye that desire me and be filled with my fruits. Blessed is the man that heareth me and that watcheth daily at my gates and waiteth at the posts of my door. He that shall find me, shall find life and have salvation from the Lord." Should it be too much to expect that we show interest in and a desire for the good things which Mary has to offer, that we watch and wait until we receive them?

Watch and wait! Her voice may reach us at any time, but it will be particularly clear and sweet on her feasts, or when we reflect on the mysteries of her life and with them also on her ways.

Watch and wait! Our Mother may keep silent and hide herself to put her children to the test. Impatience may do a great deal of harm. Let us wait until we catch the accents of her voice and feel within ourselves the glow of her love. Let us not, in our impatience for a word of consolation, run after the will-o'-

the-wisps of worldly diversions and joys. The loss would be too enormous, the disappointment too painful.

Brief as the counsel is, which the Mother of good counsel offers in the liturgy of the feast of this title, it covers all needs of the Christian life: fear and love, truth and grace, virtue and perseverance, salvation from the Lord.

# Mother of the Creator

IN THIS title the work of Christ is implicitly referred to as a creation. We speak of two creations: the first is recorded in the Book of Genesis, the second in the Gospel. The Creator in both is the same; the Son of the Blessed Virgin. Mary's divine motherhood brings her into closest relation to the second creation.

## FIRST CREATION

There is a profound, mysterious analogy between the mutual relations of the divine Persons and creation. Though creation is common to all divine Persons, we attribute some phases in it rather to one Person than to Another. Let us recall that the Son proceeds from the Father as His Word, "the brightness of His glory and the image of His substance" (Hebr. 1:3). In this image the Father beholds the infinite perfection of the divine nature; also Its infinite imitability through creation. Out of the infinite number of possible worlds which He could create, He chooses one which at the appointed moment is to become a reality. Thus the "Image of His substance" becomes the pattern; the "Word," the eternal creative fiat for all things created. "All things were made through him, and without him was made nothing that has been made" (Jn. 1:3). To the Holy Spirit we attribute the carrying out of the divine plan, culminating in the creation of man and his elevation to the supernatural order: "And God saw all the things that he had made, and they were very good" (Gen. 1:31).

The order and beauty of the first creation did not last. Sin destroyed it. Man lost the life of grace, was expelled from Paradise, and God's curse descended upon this earth. However, the designs of God cannot be thwarted. If He allows the first creation thus to be disturbed, it is because He has decreed from all eternity that another, better one, should take its place.

## Second Creation

Holy Church refers to the glory of the second creation when during holy Mass, at the mixing of wine and water, she prays, "O God, who didst create human nature in wonderful dignity and restore it more wonderful. . . ." The Creator in this new creation is the same as in the first, but now He is incarnate, having assumed the nature of man; the procedure in this second creation is not the same as in the first. In the first creation the Creator was alone; in the second creation He associates with Himself a Mother from whom He assumes human nature, so that the same nature that brought about the destruction of the first creation, might be the instrument to effect the second creation. "Oh, the depth of the riches of the wisdom and the knowledge of God! How incomprehensible are his judgments and how unsearchable his ways!" (Rom. 11:33.)

## Mother of the Creator

The second creation begins with the remaking of human nature in the Mother of the Creator. The almighty fiat of the second creation provides for her a nature that is untouched by sin, and endowed with a fullness of grace immeasurably exceeding that of the first human mother. The same almighty fiat rules out for Mary's Son a human father. The natural course of generation, by which original sin is transmitted, is not to be the way for the incarnate Word of God to enter this world. The Holy Spirit comes down upon the chosen Mother of the Creator and she conceives through the overshadowing of His love. The miraculous conception is followed by the miraculous, virginal birth of the Creator. Thus the foundation is laid and the pattern established for the new creation of man in justice and true holiness.

## CREATION PERPETUATED

The Word of God born of the Virgin Mary becomes the Head of the human race, so that all men might be renewed in Him. As He began the second creation through and with Mary, so He will continue and bring it to an end through Mary. In the moment in which the Saviour's side was pierced on the cross the Church was born. As the Creator formed the first Eve from a rib taken out of Adam's body, so the Church is formed from the body of the second Adam, who is also the Creator. But as this body had been given Him by His Mother, it is through her that He now espouses the Church to co-operate with Him in the new creation.

Through the operations of the Church the wonderful works of the second creation now begin to unfold in all their glory. By water and the Holy Spirit man is born again, "a heavenly offspring, conceived in holiness and born again as a new creature comes forth from the font's immaculate womb" (blessing of baptismal water, Holy Saturday). By means of bread and wine, changed into the body and blood of the Creator, the new life is sustained and brought to its ultimate perfection in life everlasting. All the other sacraments serve the same purpose. So all is new again, matter and spirit, earth and man, and lifted to heights which probably would never have been reached in the first creation. All this stupendous grandeur of the second creation was, according to the divine decree, to depend upon Mary. We must agree with St. Thomas when he says that the consent of the whole human race was expected in the answer of the Virgin at the Annunciation; through her the whole world received again what had been lost through the destruction of the first creation.

The second creation is everlasting; it cannot be destroyed, as was the first creation, for the whole human race, but it can be destroyed in the individual soul. May the Mother of the Creator and our Mother preserve us from such a fearful calamity.

# Mother of the Saviour

THE new creation spoken of in the preceding title is at the same time a salvation. The ruin of the first creation was such that man, left to himself, could never have repaired it. Therefore the Son of God "came down from heaven for us and our salvation" (Nicean Creed). St. Joseph is directed by an angel to call His name Jesus, "for he shall save his people from their sins" (Mt. 1:21). And the reason for the great joy announced by the angel at the birth of Jesus is that a Saviour has been born. The salvation brought to us by Jesus is deliverance from slavery, reconciliation with God, restoration of what had been lost. Mary, the Mother of the Saviour, cannot be separated from this salvation; she has given us the Saviour and she has co-operated with Him in a manner that merited for us congruously what Jesus merited condignly (Pius X, *Denz.*, 3034).

### Deliverance From Slavery

"Everyone who commits sin is a slave of sin" (Jn. 8:34). But sin being the will of Satan, the sinner becomes by it Satan's slave. What a degrading slavery it was! St. Paul thus describes it: "Now the works of the flesh are manifest, which are immorality, uncleanness, licentiousness, idolatry, witchcrafts, enmities, contentions, jealousies, anger, quarrels, factions, parties, murders, drunkenness, carousings, and such like" (Gal. 5:19). It was the realization of this misery and helplessness that called forth the burning desire and the ardent prayers for the coming of the Saviour, that we find in the Old Testament and that are still echoed in the advent liturgy of the Church, especially in the great antiphons, "Come, and with an outstretched arm redeem us — come, and bring forth from the prison house the captive that sitteth in darkness and in the shadow of death — come, and deliver man, whom Thou didst form out of the dust of the earth — come to save us, O Lord our God." Against such a background how wonderful is the love of God, of which holy Church sings in the *Exultet*, "O wondrous condescension of Thy kindness toward us, O tenderness of love beyond understanding, that to ransom a slave Thou didst give up the Son." Must we not apply the same words to the Mother of the Saviour?

### Reconciliation

What good would it have done us to be free from slavery, if we had remained excluded from the friendship of God? The fullness of redemption's blessing consists in this that we were reconciled with God, again adopted as His children and made heirs of heaven. "Christ, the Innocent, reconciled sinners with the Father (Easter Sequence). And so, "we have received a spirit of adoption of sons, by virtue of which we cry, 'Abba,

Father.' The Spirit himself gives testimony to our spirit that we are the sons of God. But if we are sons, we are heirs also, heirs indeed of God and joint heirs with Christ" (Rom. 8:15). Truly, where sin has abounded, grace has abounded more. The blessings of redemption far surpass the gifts enjoyed by our first parents in Paradise.

## THE SAVIOUR'S MOTHER

The title, Mother of the Saviour, is a title of sublime honor, and Mary paid for it as far as human labor and pain, humble, generous, self-effacing love can do so. The trials and heart-rending sorrows of her life came to her precisely because she was the Mother of the Saviour. She would not have known the poverty of Bethlehem, the fear and anxiety of her flight into Egypt, she would not have experienced the tortures of spiritual martyrdom at the sight of the cruel sufferings of Jesus and the pain and disgrace of His death, had she not been His Mother. As it is, her sorrows increase from day to day until they become a veritable avalanche rolling down upon her from the cross of her dying Son. "Holy Mary, Queen of heaven and Mistress of the world, overwhelmed with grief, stood by the cross of our Lord Jesus Christ. O all you that pass by the way, attend and see if there be any sorrow like to my sorrow" (Tract, Feast of Seven Sorrows). But co-operating with Jesus in our redemption, she also acquired a certain part ownership in its blessings. Therefore all graces and blessings of redemption reach us through her hands; she is the Mediatrix of all graces: "Our salvation is in thy hands; merely turn thy eyes to us and we shall serve the King, our Lord, with gladness" (Feast of Mediatrix of All Graces).

As long as we live here below we must co-operate with the Saviour and His Mother, working out our salvation with fear and trembling. But we must likewise co-operate in the salvation of others after the example of our heavenly Mother, who "has not spared her life by reason of the distress and tribulation of her people, but has prevented our ruin in the presence of God" (Feast of the Assumption). The price paid by the Saviour and His Mother for the salvation of souls, as well as the abundance of redemption's blessings which we have received, should arouse us to an ardent missionary zeal. But as we thus work for the salvation of others, we ever more firmly secure our own salvation, for, "My brethren, if any one of you strays from the truth, and someone brings him back, he ought to know that he who causes a sinner to be brought back from his misguided way, will save his own soul from death and will cover a multitude of sins" (James 5:19 f.).

Mother of the Saviour, help us to save our own souls and the souls of others!

# Virgin Most Prudent

IN THE parable of the wise and foolish virgins only five were prudent enough to provide themselves with sufficient oil, but even they did not have enough to help out the foolish virgins. Mary, the Virgin most prudent, waiting for the coming of the bridegroom of mankind, made her whole person, body and soul, the oil to be burned in illuminating His path; she was and is able to supply with it all those who would need and sincerely ask for it. God was so pleased with her loving watchfulness that He chose her as the sanctuary in which He would celebrate His nuptials with the human race. Mary's prudence is holy, heavenly prudence, that protects against the unholy prudence of the world and safely guides us to our eternal destiny.

PRUDENCE

Prudence, generally speaking, is the right way of doing things, considering all circumstances, in order to attain a given end. Here we speak of Christian prudence, the first of the cardinal virtues, infused together with sanctifying grace and enlightened by faith. Prudence must enter the practice of all virtues, theological and moral, and without it there can be no perfect virtue. Mary, the Queen of all saints, because of her eminent holiness and the presence of all virtues in the highest degree, must also excell all other saints by her prudence. Prudence manifests itself in our attitude toward God and created things, because this attitude is decisive for the choice we make in an individual case.

GOD THE LAST END

Even pagan wisdom gives the advice to regard the end in all things. Heavenly wisdom speaks in a similar vein: "In all thy works remember thy last end and thou shalt never sin" (Ecclus. 7:40). Even though prudence deals with what is to be done here and now, it must also take into consideration the last end. Any act that is an obstacle to the attainment of the last end is imprudent; it is the folly of exchanging the eternal for the temporal, true peace of soul for the momentary gratification of some particular desire, heaven for earth. We shall avoid such folly if, following the guidance of Christian prudence, we take the will of God as the norm of our actions. This is what Mary, the Virgin most prudent, did. The answer she gave to the angel at the Annunciation reveals her eagerness to be guided by the will of God: "Behold the handmaid of the

Lord." To be the handmaid of the Lord means to do the will of God in all things, to render perfect service. This is the purpose of man's life and it is such service that secures attainment of the last end, the blissful sentence of the Master: "Well done, good and faithful servant . . . enter into the joy of thy Master" (Mt. 25:21).

## THINGS CREATED

St. Ignatius in his Spiritual Exercises states the purpose of all created things: to help us in the attainment of our last end by giving us a better knowledge of God, increasing our love for Him, and strengthening us in His faithful service. They are all as transitory as man himself is, they come and go, and we cannot keep them forever; we must leave them behind in death. They cannot satisfy the human heart that has been made for God and is restless until it rests in God; they will forever repeat to us the warning: We are not your God. But if so, then it is prudent in each case to ask ourselves the question that guided St. Aloysius in making a choice: "What does this mean for eternity?" Nothing has any value for eternity except doing the will of God.

When men make the wrong choice they are most often led by inordinate attachments, evil passions, all stemming from the seven capital vices. Such passions are bad counselors. St. Paul says of them, "The wisdom of the flesh is hostile to God, for it is not subject to the law of God, nor can it be. And they who are carnal cannot please God" (Rom. 8:7). Christian prudence dictates that the passions be curbed and controlled.

The Blessed Virgin was free from original sin and its damaging effects on mind and will, free from the least inordinate attachment; thus she would always choose what was most pleasing to God, and that is perfect prudence.

PRAYER AND TRUST IN GOD

The human mind is limited; even where there is the proper consideration of God as our Last End, there may be many doubts and perplexities. Therefore the truly prudent man will not rely solely on his own light and judgment, but will seek light in prayer. The Virgin most prudent, therefore, must also have been most humble, acknowledging her human limitations in the knowledge of the counsels of God. There is no other supposition possible but that her habitual prayer was the supplication of our Advent liturgy: "O Wisdom, who camest out of the mouth of the Most High, reaching from end to end and ordering all things mightily and sweetly, come and teach us the way of prudence."

From the standpoint of worldly wisdom even the most prudent choice will appear frequently as folly, ever since it pleased God to save the world through the Passion of Christ — "to the Jews indeed a stumbling block, and to the Gentiles foolishness" (1 Cor. 1:21 ff.). Following the counsel of Christian prudence may cause sorrow, persecution, and death. Christian prudence will then direct our attention to the promise of the Holy Spirit, that to those who love God all things work together unto good. The final outcome will convince all of the correctness of the saints' choice and judgment. Then all those who laughed at them and ridiculed them will be forced to admit: "We fools esteemed their life madness and their end without honor; behold how they are numbered among the children of God and their lot is among the saints. Therefore we have erred . . ." (Wisd. 5:4 f.). The Virgin most prudent was unshaken in her trust in God. Not for a moment did she waver in those dark hours on Calvary in her certain expectation that Jesus would rise again; He would change death into life, sorrow into consolation, disgrace into glory. Her prudence was gloriously justified.

There is, then, convincing power in the exhortation which the Virgin most prudent addresses to us in the liturgy: "Now ye children hear me . . . Hear instruction and be wise" (Epistle, Feast of the Most Holy Rosary).

# Virgin Venerable

TO GOD we owe adoration, to the saints veneration. Canon 1276 states that, "Above all other saints the faithful should honor with filial devotion the Most Blessed Virgin Mary." Veneration is the honor and respect given to a saint because of his supernatural dignity, his virtue and consecration to a holy purpose. Sentiments of veneration call for expression and, according as such expression is public or private, we speak of the private and public veneration of the saints. In this chapter we consider the private veneration of the Virgin venerable — its basis, and the way of rendering it through invocation and imitation.

## WHY WE VENERATE MARY

We venerate the Blessed Virgin because of the stupendous supernatural gifts and favors which God has bestowed upon her: her divine motherhood, her immaculate conception and fullness of grace, her bodily assumption into heaven, the place which she holds in the economy of our salvation as Coredemptrix and Mediatrix of all graces. Mary herself acknowledges the greatness of her prerogatives in the *Magnificat*: "My soul magnifies the Lord, and my spirit rejoices in God my Saviour; because he has regarded the lowliness of his handmaid . . . because he who is mighty has done great things for me, and holy is his name" (Lk. 1:46 f.). Humility is truth; it does not ignore or deny the gifts received, but gives due credit to the Giver. God Himself cannot venerate the Blessed Virgin, since veneration implies the acknowledgment of superiority in the person venerated, but He can honor her, and He has done so far above all angels and saints. The latter, far from envying her, find in her exaltation their supreme delight and the pattern for their veneration of the most venerable of all creatures. So do all the faithful members of the Church Militant, Mary's loving children.

## INVOCATION

That it is right and salutary to invoke the saints in general, and in a particular manner the Blessed Virgin, is doctrine of our holy faith. We stand in need of grace, since without it we can do nothing to save our souls. But Mary is the Mediatrix of all graces. To turn to her with our petitions for grace and help is in no way derogatory to the divine mediatorship of Christ, but rather enhances it. We approach Him through His Mother, the most noble and holy of all creatures, whom He loves above all angels and saints. He Himself is honored by the honor we thus give to Mary. And Mary herself is pleased to present our petitions to her divine Son, knowing how much He is honored by them. Every prayer for grace is proof of the confidence which the petitioner has in Jesus and Mary, of the desire to save his soul, of his humble awareness that He cannot do so without the help of grace.

## IMITATION

True veneration leads to imitation. We cannot reasonably esteem, honor, and love the saints, unless we ourselves endeavor to become holy. St. Augustine says with regard to the martyrs, and what he says holds for all saints, "The feasts of martyrs are properly celebrated by those who follow their example; the feasts of martyrs are for us a call to martyrdom and we must not disdain to imitate what we love to celebrate" (Feast of SS. Cosmas and Damian). The sublimity of Mary's holiness is beyond our reach, but we can follow her in innumerable ways adapted to our weakness and our possibilities. We can imitate her spirit of prayer by living in the presence of God and keeping alive the desire to please Him; we can ponder on the wisdom and love of God in the salvation of the world; we can be faithful in the performance of our duties, kind to our fellow men, patient in tribulations.

Imitation is the most convincing proof of our true love and devotion to the Blessed Virgin. Imitation implies factual approval of what she has done in life; it supports and carries on the work to which she has given her life: the glorification of her divine Son. Imitation not only makes better the one who imitates the saint, but it becomes also the good example for others. It is a silent propagation of the faith, a sermon, which even the lowliest of the servants of God can preach with greater eloquence and efficacy than the most eloquent sermon delivered from the pulpit.

Honor, invocation, and imitation are the three essential elements in the veneration of the Virgin venerable; where they are present, we have true devotion to Mary, which according to Pius XII, "tends to union with Jesus under the guidance of Mary." After the canonization of St. Louis de Montfort in 1947 the Holy Father exhorted the faithful present to imitate the virtues of the saint who had distinguished himself by his devotion to the Blessed Virgin and had written a book: *True Devotion to Mary*. The Holy Father, however, felt that some clarification was needed in this matter and he added by way of caution: "The form and practice of this devotion can vary according to time, place, and personal inclination. Within the limits of sound doctrine the Church allows her children a just margin of liberty in this regard. For she realizes that a true and perfect devotion to the Blessed Virgin is never so bound to any form as to claim for itself a kind of monopoly."

Clearly, it is the will of holy Church that all good and reasonable preferences of the Christian heart in venerating the Blessed Mother of God should have their full freedom of expression. By such variety the inexhaustible wealth of Mary's greatness, power, and holiness will be brought into the realization of the faithful more effectively, and we shall behold her holiness reflected in the virtues of her children in ever new and heart-refreshing forms.

# Virgin Renowned

MARY is the *Virgo praedicanda,* the Virgin to be preached about, to be celebrated, her greatness to be proclaimed throughout the world. Not only private but also public veneration is due to her. In fact, Mary herself foretells such public veneration when, filled with the Holy Spirit, she exclaims in the *Magnificat* that all generations shall call her blessed. In this place we understand public in the wider sense, that is, as opposed to individual and private veneration. Such public veneration of the Blessed Virgin is in perfect accord with reason and faith and has found wonderful expression in the life of the Church.

## PUBLIC WORSHIP IN GENERAL

Public worship in general is an impressive profession of faith in God, His sovereign authority and providence, the glory of

His service. It is a profession of faith in an unseen world, in realities beyond those which we can see with our eyes and hear with our ears, in values exceeding all that this earth can offer. Public worship thus becomes an effective protest against the rationalistic and materialistic errors of those who would reduce man to the condition of the brute and make him seek his paradise on this earth alone: "Come therefore and let us enjoy the good things that are present . . . for this is our portion and our lot" (Wisd. 2:6).

There is inspiration in public worship. The sight of our fellow men, hundreds and thousands of them, bowing their knees in adoration, singing their hymns of praise and thanksgiving, imploring mercy in humble supplication, produces a salutary effect in all present. It is precisely the great multitude of the blessed glorifying God that will be one of the thrills experienced by the saints in heaven. Even now we feel a holy enthusiasm, so to say, as we read the description of St. John in the Apocalypse of the thousands of angels round about the throne, proclaiming with a loud voice the praises of the Lamb; or of the great multitude which no man could number out of all nations and tribes and peoples and tongues, standing before the throne and before the Lamb, crying with a loud voice, "Salvation belongs to our God . . ."; or of those hundred and forty-four thousand singing a new song and following the Lamb wherever He goes (Apoc. 5:11; 7:9; 14:1).

The public veneration of the saints is really worship offered to God, since it is through the grace of God that the saints became what they are. Moreover, the example of the saints arouses the desire of imitation. We are reminded of the deeds of the saints, of their works of piety and charity, of their courage and unselfishness, their devotion to God and the Church, their glory in heaven, of which their veneration on earth is but a faint reflection. Yet they were human like ourselves, and the grace of God that made them saints is also at our disposal; why then should we not be like them?

## Public Veneration of the Blessed Virgin

Bearing in mind that in her worship of God and the saints holy Church is guided by the Holy Spirit, we can easily see in the extraordinary, universal, and solemn veneration rendered to the Blessed Virgin by the faithful throughout the world, the special love of the Holy Spirit for His immaculate Spouse, the love of the incarnate Word of God for His Mother, the love of the Father for His most faithful daughter.

The most excellent act of liturgical worship is holy Mass. It is offered to God, but it is at the same time the greatest glorification of the Blessed Virgin. The High Priest and Victim of the eucharistic sacrifice is her divine Son. This fact alone places her in an inseparable relation to the holy sacrifice and is the reason why her name is repeatedly mentioned in every holy Mass. Moreover, a great number of feasts are celebrated in her honor; there is not a month of the year without the one or other feast of the Blessed Virgin, and some of these feasts rank among the highest of the ecclesiastical year. The formularies of the Masses and Offices for these feasts present to us in ever varying freshness and beauty the all-exceeding greatness of the Mother of God and the vital relation in which she stands to the faithful in all conditions of life.

Churches, chapels, and shrines in honor of Mary are scattered all over the earth and visited by millions of people. There is hardly a church or chapel without an altar or at least an image of the Blessed Mother of Christ. Pious practices in her honor like the recitation of the rosary, the wearing of a scapular or medal of the Blessed Virgin have been approved and encouraged by holy Church. Even though of a private nature, these practices, if followed by millions of Catholics, come to public notice and become a powerful factor for the spread of devotion to the Blessed Mother. There need be no fear that too much will ever be done in this regard, for, as Pius IX says in the Bull defining the Immaculate Conception, whatever is done in honor of Mary redounds to the honor of her Son.

By the extraordinary honor and privileges which God has conferred upon Mary He also has made known His will that she should be venerated by the faithful in an extraordinary and outstanding manner.

May the voice of praise of the children of Mary increase in volume from generation to generation until the end of time, for, as says St. Sophronius, "No one did shine like thou in the radiance of heavenly light, no one like thou has been raised above all heights. Rightly so, for no one has come as close to God as thou, no one has been enriched with gifts of God like thou. . . . Thou hast received within thyself God, the Creator and Lord of all. . . . Thou hast given Him birth, who has redeemed all men from the curse of the Father and has brought to them salvation without end."

# Virgin Powerful

THE Mother of the almighty God must be powerful. She has been chosen to co-operate with her divine Son in a work of power, that is, the liberation of an enslaved world from the tyranny of Satan and the raising of mankind from a state of misery and sin to the glory of the children of God. Mary's mission has not come to an end with her death, but will continue to the end of time. As the enemies of Christ increase in number and might, we must expect that manifestations of Mary's power will multiply until the climax arrives in the last decisive conflicts before the end of the world. Mary's power extends to the whole universe, to angels and saints and evil spirits, to God Himself since she is the suppliant omnipotence.

## Power Over Universe

We must assume that as Mother of the Creator and Queen of the universe Mary has authority over all creation and all the forces of nature. Whatever spirits, be they angels or demons, can do, Mary surely can do if it should be conducive to God's glory. She can transplant mountains and assign new courses to rivers, she can play with the stars of the sky as a child plays with a ball. In fact, this is precisely what holy Church suggests when, on the Feast of the Immaculate Conception, she applies to her the words of divine Wisdom: "I was with Him forming all things and was delighted every day, playing before Him at all times, playing in the world." The grandest manifestation of Mary's power over nature ever given to the world took place on October 13, 1917, in the stupendous sun miracle of Fatima when, "the huge ball . . . was whirling rapidly like a gigantic fire-wheel. . . . Then it rotated again, with dizzy, sickening speed. Finally there appeared on the rim a border of crimson, which flung across the sky, as from a hellish vortex, blood-red streamers of flame, reflecting to the earth, to the trees and shrubs, to the upturned faces and the clothes all sorts of brilliant colors in succession. . . . Madly gyrating in this manner three times the fiery orb seemed to tremble, to shudder, and then to plunge precipitately in a mighty zigzag toward the crowd" (Walsh, *Our Lady of Fatima*).

## Power of Authority

This power has been aptly described by the centurion in the

Gospel: "For I too am a man subject to authority, and have soldiers subject to me; and I say to one, 'Go,' and he goes; and to another, 'Come,' and he comes; and to my servant, 'Do this,' and he does it" (Mt. 8:9). It stands to reason that she, who in her immaculate conception and glorious assumption gained the most decisive victory over Satan, must always keep a commanding position in the warfare of the Church against the powers of hell. As Queen of angels and saints she is the leader of the leaders in Christ's army. When in the Garden of Olives Peter undertook to defend his Master by the use of violence, Jesus told him to put back his sword into the scabbard: "Or dost thou suppose I cannot entreat my Father, and he will even now furnish me with more than twelve legions of angels?" (Mt. 26:53.) These legions of angels are also at the command of their Queen. As God wills and the conditions of the time call for it, she will make use of her authority.

POWER OF INTERCESSION

Mary is called the suppliant omnipotence. As Mother of Jesus she exercised authority over Him during His earthly life and He fulfilled her every wish; will He do less for her now? It is as if He says to her: "Ask, My Mother; it would not be right that I should turn thee away" (Antiphon, Feast of Mediatrix of All Graces). Holy Scripture records but one instance of Mary's power of intercession, but it is most significant. It was at the wedding feast of Cana; Mary noticed that the supply of wine was giving out. It was clear at once that no one but Jesus could help. Without any explanation Mary approaches Him with the simple words, "They have no wine." The answer of Jesus is a splendid justification of His Mother's trust. Let us imagine how Jesus looks at His Mother, His eyes speaking more eloquently than His words: "Woman, do you realize what this occasion and your petition mean for Me and for you?

The hour set by My Father for My manifestation through the working of miracles has not yet come, but you have speeded its coming through your intercession." And Jesus changes water into wine. Mary's power of intercession has not diminished since that day, and the history of the Church proves that there is nothing impossible for the Mother of Christ.

As Jesus in the love of His Sacred Heart is rich for all who call upon Him, so Mary in her power is rich for all who invoke her. Provided we acknowledge our weakness and ask for help, there is nothing that Mary could and would not do, if it serves the best interests of our soul. That the saints, in spite of human weakness, became what they are is due, next to God, to the powerful intercession and help of Mary. Her power is meant also for us. We are fearful and often feel forsaken by friends with no one to understand us; we look into the future with dread forebodings, especially in view of the threatening signs of the times. We need a profounder realization that the Virgin powerful, mightier than all the powers of hell, is on our side, protecting us. Let Satan's emissaries sound the trumpet for the attack, let fists be clenched and armies march, let them threaten the followers of Christ with enslavement, torture, and death, let them hurl their defiant blasphemies at God and His holy Mother. The Almighty laughs at them; He will break their power and destroy them when the time has come, and He will do it through the Virgin powerful.

# Virgin Merciful

THE power of the Virgin powerful finds its complement, in a way, in the kindness and mercy of her motherly heart; her power stands in the service of mercy. Mercy inclines to help in need, to forgive, to return good for evil. It cannot be otherwise with Mary, since she is the most distinguished daughter of the Father of mercies; in her beats the Heart of Jesus patient and most merciful, and as Spouse of the Spirit of Love she must be all aflame with divine love.

## DAUGHTER OF THE FATHER

God is love. His love urged Him to communicate His gifts to beings capable of knowing and loving Him, and therefore He created man according to His image and likeness. But He wished to be not only their Creator but their Father as well: "Behold what manner of love the Father has bestowed upon us, that we should be called children of God; and such we are" (1 Jn. 3:1). With fatherly love He takes care of all their natural needs, providing them with food and clothing and shelter and whatever else they might need. Even more impressive is the Father's concern for the spiritual welfare of His children. He wants them to be holy as He is holy, so as to make themselves worthy of their heavenly inheritance. He is eager even to forgive their sins. He pleads with the sinner to return to Him and promises forgiveness: "If the wicked do penance for all his sins . . . he shall live and shall not die. I will not remember all his iniquities . . . O house of Israel . . . be converted and do penance . . . and iniquity shall not be your ruin. . . . For I desire not the death of him that dieth . . . return ye and live" (Ezech. 18:21 ff.). Indeed, the mercy of God is above all His works.

The mercy of the Father overflowed into the heart of Mary when she became the Mother of His eternal Son, with such abundance as to make it an inexhaustible source from which all men will be able to draw to the end of time.

## MOTHER OF THE SON

If there was ever identity of love and desire between two hearts we find it in Jesus and Mary. But Jesus became her Son that He might be the Saviour of the world. Jesus is the Good Shepherd who seeks the lost sheep and in the end lays down His life for them. No one is excluded from His mercy and He invites all who labor and are burdened to come to Him; He will refresh them, He will give peace to their hearts. Mary had opportunity to observe the Saviour's love for men from the days of His infancy through the many years of prayer, work, and obedience at Nazareth. She was with Him in thought and sentiment during the labors, disappointments, and sufferings of His public life. She stood beneath the cross and heard Christ's last seven words, outpourings of merciful love. In the presence of such overpowering manifestations of merciful love Mary's heart cannot but expand more and more, "to comprehend what is the breadth and length and height and depth, and to know Christ's love which surpasses knowledge" (Eph. 3:18). Will she not use all her power and influence over the Heart of Jesus to obtain forgiveness for the sinner, and grace that will lead him back into the arms of his heavenly Father? And if there is joy in heaven over one sinner doing penance more than over ninety-nine just who have not sinned, then at the head of all those rejoicing stands the Virgin merciful.

## SPOUSE OF THE HOLY SPIRIT

Whatever gifts were bestowed upon men were bestowed in and through the love of the Holy Spirit. The Holy Spirit stands at the beginning and the end of the work of redemption. Mary conceived the incarnate Word of God through the Holy Spirit, and it was in the same Spirit that Jesus offered Himself to the Father as immaculate victim. It is through the Holy

Spirit that we were born again in baptism, received forgiveness of sin in the sacrament of penance, and expect the things God has prepared for those who love Him, because, "to us God has revealed them through his Spirit" (1 Cor. 2:9). Our hope of salvation is inseparably bound up with the Holy Spirit, but, "hope does not disappoint, because charity of God is poured forth in our hearts by the Holy Spirit who has been given to us" (Rom. 5:5).

Mary is the immaculate Spouse of the Holy Spirit. The first and foremost gift of spouses to each other is their love, their own self: "My beloved to me and I to him" (Cant. 2:16). But, if the Holy Spirit gives Himself to Mary, penetrating and filling the very substance of her soul and body with His love, what then must be the love of the Virgin merciful! There is but one conclusion possible: there can be no human person that loves souls more than she, none that does more for the conversion of sinners than the Virgin merciful.

There is something wonderfully soothing in the thought that there is one who always thinks kindly of us, who will not condemn after we have failed, but will seek to excuse and consider all mitigating circumstances, one who will plead for time to repent and to do penance for deeds that cannot be excused. The Virgin merciful does all this for us and much more. She stays the hand of divine justice, hoping to the last for a response to her motherly pleading on the part of the sinner. Patient and merciful love is needed to save the world, and that is the thought to be remembered by all the children of Mary, who together with her would work for the salvation of souls. Love clothed in kindness, sympathy, patience, will draw souls thirsting for love to the loving Heart of Jesus and to Mary, the Virgin merciful.

# Virgin Faithful

BY OUR very nature we are servants of God. Divine Providence has assigned to each one a definite task in life and for its accomplishment bestowed upon him all necessary gifts and qualifications. These gifts of God are precious and must not be squandered or left unused, as was the talent buried in the ground by the unprofitable servant. In the use of these gifts man must prove himself a faithful servant, administering his Master's goods according to His will. Mary, the humble handmaid of the Lord, is the sublimest exemplar of fidelity for all servants of God. Faithful service is rendered to God in particular through baptismal and religious fidelity, and under these two aspects we will consider the Virgin faithful.

## BAPTISMAL FIDELITY

Baptism is the beginning of our Christian life. We were raised to the dignity of children of God, endowed with stupendous gifts and given a definite task, and we on our part assumed definite obligations. We renounced Satan and all his works and all his pomps, and pledged ourselves to the observance of God's commandments. The works of Satan are sin in every form and shape, the pomps of Satan are the glitter and tinsel of worldly display, of lawless and riotous feasting and sensual enjoyment. We cannot serve two masters, we cannot serve Satan and God. Every sin is work rendered in the service of Satan, and therefore a breach of the promises made at baptism. Every failure to live up to the obligations assumed, connivance at un-Christian principles, fraternization with the enemy of God, is infidelity, treason more or less.

Mary's immaculate conception and fullness of grace were, in a sense, her baptism. There was no need for her to renounce Satan, since by her very endowments and office she was marked as the woman who would crush the serpent's head. Mary accepted the office assigned to her, placing herself absolutely and unconditionally at the disposal of God when she answered, "Behold the handmaid of the Lord; be it done to me according to thy word" (Lk. 1:38). These words were the baptismal promises of the Blessed Virgin, and she kept them with unparalleled fidelity. There is not a trace in her of Satan's works and pomps. She lives as the handmaid of the Lord and loves unto death; and faithful unto death she earns the crown of life. Thus the Virgin faithful was the worthy Mother of Jesus Christ, who is "the faithful witness" (Apoc. 1:5), called "faithful and true" (Apoc. 19:11).

RELIGIOUS FIDELITY

Beyond the life of the ordinary Christian, be it in the single or the married state, there is a higher form of life. The religious state is the answer to a divine call and invitation, not a command or threat of punishment. The liberty to accept or reject the call is now left to the individual in precisely the same manner in which it was left to the young man to whom Jesus addressed the words, "If thou wilt be perfect, go, sell what thou hast and give to the poor, and thou shalt have a treasure in heaven; and come, follow me" (Mt. 19:21). However, with the acceptance of the call goes the acceptance of certain definite obligations. The religious binds himself to strive after higher perfection through the observance of the vows of poverty, chastity, and obedience, and the observance of the constitutions of his respective institute. The test of religious fidelity is not the taking of the vows on the day of profession but their observance, the daily dying to one's own will in order to do the will of God ever more perfectly.

The Blessed Virgin was not a religious, yet she is the most perfect and inspiring model of religious fidelity. The degree of perfection is proportionate to the degree of surrender to the will of God. There can be no more complete and perfect surrender than that of the Virgin faithful. As a young girl she had taken the vow of virginity in order that she might give all her love to God; her love and practice of poverty and obedience exceeded that of any religious. There is compelling reason to believe private revelations which tell us that Mary gave away whatever was not necessary for life and that in the management of her little household she was delighted to fulfill and even anticipate the wishes of St. Joseph. She lived in the fullest conformity with the will of God in whatsoever way it might be made known to her. And so religious perfection is nothing but the unwavering persistent fidelity in doing the will of God.

There are three signs by which we can judge to what extent we approach the ideal of our heavenly Mother, whether as simple Christians or as religious.

Surrender to God's will must be complete; there can be no exceptions or reservations made in keeping our promises, baptismal or religious. All our thoughts and words and deeds, all the love of our hearts must be given to God, all obligations must be fulfilled faithfully. God accepts no divided allegiance. Furthermore, full surrender to the will of God admits of no conditions to make the service of God dependent upon circumstances of time, place, or environment. Lastly, service must be lifelong; it cannot be limited to a certain number of years, to the one or other period of life.

Amid the general relaxation of moral restraints and the lowering of moral standards, baptismal and religious fidelity must become a beacon light showing to the world the duty and honor, peace and glory of fidelity in the service of God. By the grace of God and the help and intercession of the Virgin faithful it is possible. "I am convinced of this, that he who has begun a good work in you will bring it to perfection until the day of Christ Jesus" (Phil. 1:16).

# Mirror of Justice

JUSTICE in scriptural language denotes faithful observance of the law of God, perfection of life. Thus St. Joseph is called a just man, and the parents of St. John the Baptist "were just before God, walking blamelessly in all the commandments and ordinances of the Lord" (Lk. 1:16). The commandments of God and any other manifestation of His will are often called a light or lamp. This light of God falls upon us and we like a mirror are to reflect it in the conduct of our life. Because Mary did this in the most perfect manner she is called the Mirror of justice. She acts in everything according to God's holy will, in regard to God, in regard to herself, and in regard to her fellow men.

## In Regard to God

God demands of us faith, hope, love, and obedient service. In our faith we reflect God's truth, in hope His fidelity, in love and service His holiness.

Mary's life is a life of faith. She believed all that God had revealed; she believed the prophecies concerning the Messias and prayed for His coming. Thus she was prepared for the greatest act of faith in her life, faith in the stupendous miracle of the Incarnation to be accomplished in her; she herself was to be the Virgin Mother of Emmanuel, as foretold by Isaias. Well could Elizabeth call her blessed because of this faith: "Blessed is she who has believed, because the things promised her by the Lord shall be accomplished" (Lk. 1:45). Faith inspired Mary's hope. God's fidelity would carry out what He had promised. Her hope increased with leaps and bounds, when after the Annunciation she realized that the greatest of all prophecies had been fulfilled in her own person. Now all her thoughts and desires center in the incarnate Word of God; she immerses her soul into the soul of Jesus and consumes her life in His loving service, as He fulfills the task assigned to Him by His heavenly Father of redeeming the world. Thus she becomes the perfect reflection of God's love and holiness. And so the Christian life must reflect the will of God by believing what He has revealed, by hoping for what He has promised, by doing what He commands or desires. Then will the world have an illustration of the wonderful beauty, harmony, peace, and blessing of a life according to the will of God.

## In Regard to Self

God has imposed duties upon us, many and grave duties, all converging in the paramount obligation of saving our souls, for "what would it profit a man if he gain the whole world, but suffer the loss of his soul?" Christ wants us to be perfect because our Father in heaven is perfect, and St. Paul states definitely: "This is the will of God, your sanctification" (1 Thess. 4:3). Since we are sanctified by doing the will of God, this particular obligation of striving after perfection extends to the fulfillment of the whole law. A higher type of self-love will aim at fulfilling not only the commands but also the wishes of God as proposed in the religious state. The very fact that this state is the following of an invitation, not of a command, points to the eminent degree of God-willed self-love. The religious follows in the footsteps of Jesus as closely as is possible in this life; there can be nothing that gives to man greater distinction and worth.

Mary is the mirror of such justice. God had loved her above all angels and saints — should she not love herself? She guarded the gifts received, co-operated with them through the most generous surrender of her will to the will of God. The slightest wish of God is command for her. Thus she is "the brightness of eternal light and the unspotted mirror of God's majesty, and the image of His goodness" (Feast of the Most Pure Heart of Mary).

## In Regard to Fellow Men

St. Paul writes to the Romans, "Owe no man anything except to love one another; for he who loves his neighbor has fulfilled the law. . . . And if there is any other commandment, it is summed up in this saying, 'Thou shalt love thy neighbor as thyself.' Love does no evil to a neighbor. Love therefore is the fulfillment of the law" (Rom. 13:8 f.). Love of neighbor reflects the charity of God, by which Jesus has shed His blood for the salvation of men and called them to a share in His own nature and glory.

Mary, loving God as she did, must have loved men with greater love than all angels and men combined. St. Alphonsus says, "Never did a created person exist, nor could there exist such a person, that loved God with greater love than Mary. For the same reason there was not nor could there be any created being that could love his fellow men more than Mary did." Thus her whole life, as it stands in the service of her divine Son, also stands in the service of men; it is one grand act of charity. She loved unto death, and for that reason she is the most perfect reflection of that divine love by which God "has not spared even his own Son, but has delivered him for us all" (Rom. 8:32). Love of God and love of neighbor are inseparable; there can be no true love of God without love of neighbor, for, "if any one says, 'I love God,' and hates his brother, he is a liar. For how can he, who does not love his brother whom he sees, love God, whom he does not see?" (1 Jn. 4:20.) True love of neighbor is justice, justice which sanctifies, for it is patient and kind, does not envy, thinks no evil, bears with all things, endures all things.

Mary, the Mirror of justice, reflects most perfectly the holiness of God. Let us look at this heavenly reflection, that our hearts may be inflamed with holy love and aroused to imitation. Surely, if all Christians, all religious, like millions of mirrors would reflect the light of Christian life and holiness in the world, darkness would be changed into light, and Christ, the King of justice, would rule over mankind.

# Seat of Wisdom

WISDOM is prudence in the most eminent sense. Prudence considers the proximate end, wisdom aims at the last end. Wisdom attains its highest perfection through the gift of wisdom, which adds a certain relish to the practice of virtue and thus powerfully and sweetly attracts the soul to God. The Virgin most prudent, possessing the gifts of the Holy Spirit in the highest degree, must for this reason also be the Virgin most wise. Mary is called the Seat of wisdom, because she is the Mother of the incarnate divine Wisdom, possessed and practiced wisdom in the highest degree, and is so to say the storehouse and supply station of whatever wisdom we need for the attainment of our last end.

## Divine Wisdom

Divine wisdom was active in creation and in the whole economy of man's redemption. Angels and men and everything else created were to be raised up to God in a mysterious manner through the incarnation of the second Person of the Most Blessed Trinity, the subsistent divine Wisdom, the Word of God. St. Paul dwells on this idea and complements it when he writes: "All things have been created through him and unto him, and he is before all creatures, and in him all things hold together" (Col. 1:17). The words of the Apostle give us a glimpse into the divine purpose of creation. Material creation was to furnish the material for the human body of the God-man, and the whole spiritual creation, angels and human souls, were to reach the highest perfection in the human soul of the incarnate Word of God, "the firstborn of every creature."

Mary, through the part assigned to her in the eternal decrees of our salvation, stands next to her divine Son, the incarnate divine Wisdom. For this reason she must be presumed to possess a profounder understanding of creation's purpose than any angel or man. Holy Church suggests as much when she applies to her the words predicated of divine Wisdom: "When he prepared the heavens I was there; when with a certain law and compass he enclosed the depths . . . I was with Him forming all things" (Prov. 8:22). We can say that the Mother of God accompanies divine Wisdom as It calls the universe into existence and understands why things are created. Human minds have been able to discover much of the purpose of creation and were inflamed with love of the Creator. How much more clearly must *she* have recognized the purpose of creation, whose mind had never been darkened by the shadow of sin, whose will had never been weakened by any inordinate passion.

More impressively yet does divine Wisdom shine forth in the economy of our salvation. It was accomplished by means which, according to the standards of the world, would never have been considered suitable for the attainment of such an end. Let us think of the poverty of Christ's birth and the lowliness of His hidden life, the sufferings and humiliations of His death. But according to St. Paul there is revealed in the Passion of Christ the power and the wisdom of God. Is it not a postulate of sound reason to assume that Mary, so closely associated with Jesus in the accomplishment of our redemption, must have penetrated into the mysteries of this power and wisdom beyond the reach of any angel or saint?

## WISDOM OF THE WORLD

Divine wisdom stands in irreconcilable opposition to the wisdom of the world. Of this latter wisdom St. Paul says, "While professing themselves wise they have become fools and they have changed the glory of the incorruptible God for an image like to corruptible man and to birds and four-footed beasts and creeping things" (Rom. 1:23). This ignoring and perverting of the primary purpose of creation holds not only for the degrading aberrations of idolatry, but also for the atheism and secularism of our times. The fundamental folly of worldly wisdom consists in this that it leaves the ultimate end entirely out of consideration and evaluates the goods of this earth not according to the principles of reason and faith, but according to the expediency and pleasure of the moment. All too many Christians are infected with this wisdom of the world. They stand in need of reorientation, and they will find it with Mary, the Seat of wisdom. The highest type of wisdom is to be a faithful servant of God as Mary was His humble handmaid.

## The Gift of Wisdom

The virtue of wisdom is perfected through the gift of wisdom. It is infused into the soul together with sanctifying grace. Since the gift of wisdom imparts a certain delight in divine things and to the same extent lessens attachment to created things, the gift of wisdom is a wonderful help in the practice of virtue and the pursuance of Christian perfection. Wherever a holy life is flourishing, in service rendered to God in the joy and gladness of the heart, we behold the effects of the gift of wisdom. Wisdom indeed is "an infinite treasure to men, which they that use it become the friends of God" (Wisd. 7:14). Mary being full of grace must have possessed the gift of wisdom in the highest degree. As our Mother she is most desirous that her children should be wise — wise with the wisdom of the Holy Spirit that is made known to us in the commandments and counsels of God.

A particular reason that should compel us to seek true wisdom is the frightful bankruptcy of worldly wisdom which our days have witnessed. It promised to men an earthly paradise, but it has changed earth to a place of horror, fear and hunger, misery and despair, wherever it has had its way. It is then a timely and practical prayer for heavenly wisdom to pray with the Church: to despise the things of earth and to love those of heaven — to love what God commands and to desire what He promises, so that amid the changing conditions of life our hearts may dwell where true joys abide. It shall be given us through Mary, the Seat of wisdom.

# Cause of Our Joy

THE times of the Messias are pictured by the prophets as times of abundance, peace, and joy: "You shall draw waters with joy out of the Saviour's fountains" (Isa. 12:3). When Jesus was born, His birth was announced by the angels as news of great joy. Holy Church sees cause for joy in the Christmas mystery, when she prays at the Offertory of the first Mass, "Let the heavens rejoice and the earth be glad before the face of the Lord, because He has come." But there would be no Messias, no birth of Christ without His Mother. Next to Jesus, Mary is the Cause of our joy, and holy Church acknowledges this fact when on the Feast of Mary's Nativity she sings, "Thy birth, O Blessed Virgin, has brought joy to the whole world." The principal joys which we draw through Mary from the fountains of the Saviour are the adoption of sons, holiness of life, and heavenly glory.

## ADOPTION OF SONS

The adoption of sons presupposes forgiveness of sins; but Jesus is the Lamb of God, that has taken away the sins of the world. "Indeed, he has taken it completely away, nailing it to the cross" (Col. 2:14). Even after sin has been forgiven joy would not be complete, unless we were reinstated into the ranks of the children of God, who can expect heaven as their legitimate inheritance. Man had lost the divine sonship and, helpless and hopeless, he spent his days away from his Father's home. It was a terrible loss. Time did not heal this wound which sin had inflicted, but rather increased its pain. But what a change has come over us. St. Paul writes, "You have received a spirit of adoption as sons, by virtue of which we cry, 'Abba, Father.' The Spirit himself gives testimony to our spirit that we are the sons of God. But if we are sons, we are heirs also, heirs indeed of God and joint heirs with Christ" (Rom. 8:15 f.).

Mary has given us the Lamb of God that takes away the sins of the world; and are we not the children of God because, incorporated as members into the mystical body of her divine Son, we are her spiritual children?

## HOLINESS OF LIFE

It must have been news of profoundest joy for the Ephesians when they read the words the great Apostle had written to them, "You are no longer strangers and foreigners, but you are citizens with the saints and members of Christ's household" (Eph. 2:19). Holiness of life and with it the glory of the saints is within our reach. The saints became saints through the grace which is also at our disposal; they are the heralds of God's mercy and the power of His grace. Merely to think of them devoutly inspires holy desires; their courage and zeal overflow into our hearts, knowing that with the help of grace we too can become holy.

At the head of all saints, as the glory of Jerusalem, the joy of Israel, and the honor of all mankind, stands the Queen of all saints, the Cause of their and our joy. Not only is her intercession more powerful than that of any other saint, but there is in her example the sweet and gentle appeal of motherly love. She knows best how to guide and encourage, to attract and to support, how to arouse heavenly desires and generous resolutions. The more we love and invoke Mary, the more rapid will be our progress in holiness. Jesus cannot but love and favor those whom He sees loving and being loved by His holy Mother. So Mary is our sweetness, our hope, and, more than any other saint, the Cause of our joy.

## HEAVENLY GLORY

Where suffering and abandonment loom on the horizon, where the future looks dark without a silver lining, there can be no joy. Such a condition is impossible for the believing Christian. The glorious prospects which faith holds out to him are strong enough not only to make suffering bearable, but to fill the soul with joy in the midst of tribulations, for with the Apostle we also "reckon that the sufferings of the present time are not worthy to be compared with the glory to come that will be revealed in us" (Rom. 8:18). Holy Church speaks of heaven as refreshment, light, and peace. The saints shall not hunger and thirst any more, for they shall drink from the fountains of life; light brighter than the sun shall illumine their heavenly abode and banish night forever, for the Lamb shall be the lamp of the heavenly city; peace profound because without any fear of being ever disturbed, shall inundate their hearts. And who will describe the joy derived from the company of the saints, now free from human shortcomings, serenely reflecting the perfection and amiability of God!

Yet these glorious prospects would not be ours without Mary the Cause of our joy. As Coredemptrix she merited for us congruously what Jesus merited condignly. And she is ever active in behalf of our salvation by her intercession, by the heavenly desires which she arouses in the soul, by the hope which she enkindles, by the help with which she lightens our burdens. Let us add, that she is also the Mother of our Judge; could her divine Son condemn to hell one for whom His holy Mother intercedes? St. Alphonsus and numberless doctors of the Church insist that one who loves and venerates Mary shall never be lost.

The prospect of seeing our heavenly Mother face to face and of spending our eternity with her is one of the brightest lights in our joy. Indeed, heaven would not be heaven without her. Until we are with her in heaven, safe in our Father's home and drawing the waters of joy from the eternal fountains of the Saviour, Mary is the Cause of our hope and joy. "And after this our exile show us the blessed fruit of thy womb, Jesus. O clement, O loving, O sweet Virgin Mary."

# Spiritual Vessel

SENDING Ananias to Saul after the latter's vision at the gate of Damascus, Jesus speaks of the future Apostle as a vessel: "Go, for this man is a chosen vessel to me, to carry my name among nations and kings and the children of Israel" (Acts 9:15). In like manner does the Apostle later speak of himself as a vessel: "But we carry this treasure in vessels of clay, to show that the abundance of the power is God's and not ours" (2 Cor. 4:7). His treasure is the Gospel of Christ and his call to the apostolate. The Blessed Virgin is called a Spiritual Vessel, that is, the Vessel of the Holy Spirit, because the Holy Spirit gave Himself to her and deposited in her spiritual gifts surpassing in excellence and abundance those of any other created being. She is not a vessel of clay sharing in the moral frailty of man, but a Spiritual Vessel free from any inordinate stirring of corrupt nature. Let us consider now the operation of the seven gifts of the Holy Spirit in her soul and draw some practical lessons from it.

## The Seven Gifts

What the prophet foretold of the Messias holds also for Mary within the limits of her capacity: "And the Spirit of the Lord shall rest upon him: the spirit of wisdom and understanding, the spirit of counsel and fortitude, the spirit of knowledge and godliness, and he shall be filled with the spirit of the fear of the Lord" (Isa. 11:2). The purpose of these seven gifts is to make the soul ever more sensitive to the inspirations of the Holy Spirit and prompt in their execution.

The fear of the Lord makes us see the malice of sin for what it really is: the greatest evil in the world, because it is a rebellion against the all-powerful and holy will of God, an alliance with God's implacable enemy, the cause of man's eternal ruin; all this cannot but arouse a profound hatred of sin. Mary saw the work of sin in the sufferings of her divine Son and she must have trembled at the very thought of sin.

Piety shows us God as our infinitely good and loving Father, draws us to God, keeps us remembering His presence, arouses love of prayer and spiritual things. Piety draws Mary to the Temple even as a child, makes her ponder over the mysteries of God and rejoice in His presence and love.

Knowledge gives us the correct evaluation of created things and makes us indifferent toward them, ready to give them up whenever the honor of God or the good of our souls calls for it. Mary's freedom from the effects of original sin excluded any inordinate attachment to created things, and her happiness in poverty and privation, her readiness to give up all she had in order to be the handmaid of the Lord are proofs of it.

Fortitude makes us strong to do and endure great things for God. Greatness does not depend upon external appearance and the applause of men but upon love, forgetfulness of self. All things done by Mary were great; and the greater, the less spectacular they were, because her love was so great, exceeding all thought and imagination. As Queen of martyrs she suffered more than all martyrs and saints combined. The never failing courage and patience in her suffering are the fruit of the gift of fortitude.

The gift of counsel shows us the will of God in doubts and difficulties. Face to face with the decrees and mysteries of infinite wisdom and love, Mary too stood in need of counsel. The questions she asked at the Annunciation and at the finding of Jesus in the Temple, her pondering over the things she had seen and heard, show her seeking counsel. That she acted at all times as the Virgin most prudent, that she became the Mother of good counsel for her children, is due to the gift of counsel.

Understanding opens up for us wonderful vistas into the mysteries of our holy faith, their depth and beauty and significance for our lives. Through her motherhood Mary had entered a most intimate relation to the three Persons of the Most Blessed Trinity. Through her the Father sent His only-begotten Son into the world; the Son assumed human nature; the Holy Spirit made her the Mother of Christ. And all this in order to atone for sin and to save souls. Mary was, so to speak, the confidante of the three divine Persons. Could we assume that she, who played such an important part in all these mysteries, was not given the most profound understanding of them?

Wisdom partakes in the nature and effects of all the other gifts. Its characteristic feature is that it arouses joy and gladness in the service of God. The fullness in which Mary possessed the other gifts allows us to make definite conclusions as to the fullness of the gift of wisdom in her. She experienced the truth of what the wise man said: "Now all good things came to me together with her and innumerable riches through her hand, and I rejoiced in all these" (Wisd. 7:11). Mary's *Magnificat* is the fruit and glorifications of the seven gifts of the Holy Spirit.

LESSONS

As children of Mary we too are and must be spiritual vessels. The Holy Spirit took up His abode in our souls in baptism and brought with Him the seven gifts as a birthday present; He perfected these gifts in confirmation and whenever we received an increase of sanctifying grace. We have become partakers in the divine nature; yet God is a Spirit, and partaking in His nature must spiritualize our nature and life. And so, according to the Apostle, we are no longer debtors of the flesh so as to live according to the flesh, but debtors of the Holy Spirit so as to live in Him.

These thoughts on Mary as the Spiritual Vessel should give us a greater awareness and appreciation of the wonderful gifts which the Holy Spirit has put into our souls, and of the heights of spirituality that have come within our reach. Like Mary the Spiritual Vessel, we too can be vessels, "filled with the Holy Spirit, speaking to one another in psalms and hymns and spiritual songs, singing and making melody in your hearts to the Lord, giving thanks always for all things in the name of our Lord Jesus Christ to God the Father" (Eph. 5:19 f.).

# Vessel of Honor

AS SPIRITUAL VESSEL, filled with the Holy Spirit and His precious gifts, Mary is also a Vessel of honor. But this title penetrates more deeply than the preceding one into the mysterious designs of the Holy Spirit; He made Mary a Spiritual Vessel of such surpassing excellence, because she was to hold the flesh and blood of the incarnate Word of God. We will get a more definite idea of the richness of this title when we consider the honor due to sacred vessels used for the offering of holy Mass and the preservation of the Blessed Sacrament. Their material, form, and consecration throw a wonderful light on the honor due to the living and most sacred of all sacred vessels, Mary, the Vessel of honor.

### MATERIAL

Only the most precious materials are to be used for sacred vessels: gold, silver, precious stones. At least those parts which come into immediate contact with the sacred species must be gold. For the living Vessel of honor the Holy Spirit Himself prepared the material, since in the whole of creation no suitable material could be found. Mary's soul was created in the state of sanctifying grace, her body exempt from the effects of original sin; it was to be free from any ingredients of evil lust, sparkling in the luster of purity and love undefiled. Moreover, this material was to be used not only for the making of the vessel itself, but also for the fashioning of its contents, for, "blessed is the womb of the Virgin Mary that bore the Son of the eternal Father, and blessed are the breasts that gave suck to Christ the Lord, who on this day deigned to be born of the Virgin for the salvation of the world" (Christmas Office, third nocturn).

### FORM

The form given to sacred vessels is different from that of profane vessels; it marks them at once as destined for a sacred purpose. So St. Paul wants the Christians to be different from their pagan neighbors; they should assume the form of Christ, be transformed into Christ, "for those whom he has foreknown, he has also predestined to be conformed to the image of his son" (Rom. 8:29). And the prayer of the Church in the first Christmas Mass is that "we may be found in the form of Him, in whom our nature is united with Thee." The Holy Spirit impressed upon Mary the form of Christ that she in turn might give it to her divine Son. The great Apostle describes this form of Christ as "taking the nature of a slave and being made like unto men. And appearing in the form of man, he humbled himself, becoming obedient to death, even to death on a cross" (Phil. 2:7). Again he speaks of the form of Christ in the epistle to the Hebrews as, "a high priest, holy, innocent, undefiled, set apart from sinners, and become higher than the heavens" (Hebr. 7:26). Do we not recognize in this description of the Apostle the form of Christ's Mother, the Vessel of honor? She is the humble handmaid of the Lord, obedient unto death, holy, innocent, undefiled, higher than all the angels and saints. There were saints whose outward appearance bore the imprint of heavenliness and raised the thoughts and aspirations of their fellow men to heavenly things; could we expect less of her, who was the most perfect double of the form of Christ?

CONSECRATION

Before chalice and paten may be used for their sacred purpose they must be consecrated. Such consecration bestows upon the vessels a certain sacredness that fits them for their use. Yet, in the case of material vessels the consecration does not change their nature, nor does it enter their substance, so that under circumstances their consecration may be lost. Mary, the Vessel of honor, was consecrated by the Holy Spirit in her immaculate conception and again at the Annunciation with a consecration that changed her very substance, entered her innermost being, and for that reason cannot be lost. The gold of her love never wears off; she is impervious to any deteriorating influence. She is always the Vessel of honor, because always the Spouse of the Holy Spirit and the Mother of Christ.

The Christian, too, is a vessel of honor. We have been chosen, set aside, and consecrated for the service of God in baptism and confirmation; we are the vessels of the flesh and blood of Mary's Son in Holy Communion, and at all times we are to be Christ-bearers, to whom the Apostle proposes the motto: "Glorify God and bear him in your body" (1 Cor. 6:20). Therefore, "be not conformed to this world, but be transformed in the newness of your mind" (Rom. 12:2). Though in the world, we must not be of the world; we must be different from it: our mentality, our outlook on life, our words and deeds must give evidence of our consecration, of the presence of God within us. We are vessels of honor because we are vessels of God.

# Singular Vessel of Devotion

AS SPOUSE of the Holy Spirit, filled with His presence and His wonderful gifts, Mary is the Spiritual Vessel; as Mother of the incarnate Word of God she becomes the Vessel of honor, the chalice and paten holding the flesh and blood of the Lamb of God. Conscious of her exaltation and the unique place assigned to her in the redemption of the world Mary consecrates herself to the Father in absolute and unconditional self-surrender. Such self-surrender is devotion in the strict sense of the word; it is fostered by recollection and spiritual fervor, is productive of spiritual joy and consolation, and all this is devotion in the wider sense of the word. Because Mary possessed all these forms of devotion in a supereminent degree, she is called the Singular Vessel of devotion.

Devotion

Devotion in the sense of self-oblation is the reaction of the heart to the realization that God is our Creator, Lord, and Last End, the Giver of all that we are and possess. All must be returned to Him by being used for His glory. The highest expression of such devotion we find in our blessed Saviour. According to the prophet He enters the world with the words, "Sacrifice and oblation thou wouldst not, but a body thou hast fitted to me. . . . Behold, I come . . . to do thy will" (Hebr. 9:5). Thus Jesus offers Himself to the Father for the mission entrusted to Him, which eventually will terminate with His death on the cross. We find the most perfect counterpart of this act of devotion in the words of Mary addressed to the angel, "Behold the handmaid of the Lord; be it done to me according to thy word" (Lk. 1:38). She asks and answers, as it were, the question of the psalmist, "What shall I render to the Lord for all the things that he hath rendered to me? I will take the chalice of salvation, and I will call upon the name of the Lord. I will pay my vows to the Lord before all his people" (Ps. 115:3). This chalice of salvation is Mary, the Mother of the divine Victim, and beneath the cross she pays her vows to the Lord in the sight of His people. Then and there she proved herself to be the Singular Vessel of devotion.

Devotion in the sense of self-oblation is implied in the very idea of the Christian life. In baptism we died to ourselves in order to live for God. To live for God means to live according to faith, to profess the faith even unto a martyr's death. Absence or deficiency of such devotion is the explanation for all defections from grace and faith, particularly for so much mediocrity in the Christian life. Imitation of Mary's devotion will bring about a change.

## RECOLLECTION

A loving concentration of the mind on God and things divine, which is recollection, gives us a deeper understanding of the reasonableness, necessity, and glory of self-oblation and secures grace for its practice. It is one of the principal factors in the attainment of Christian perfection. Mary surpassed all saints in the spirit of recollection. After the departure of the shepherds, "Mary kept in mind all these words, pondering them in her heart" (Lk. 2:19); again, after the finding of Jesus in the Temple, "his mother kept all these things carefully in her heart" (Lk. 2:52). For many years Mary was face to face with the mysteries of divine love as they unfolded in the life of her divine Son, particularly in His Passion, Resurrection, and Ascension: infinite self-abasement, humiliation, and suffering beyond expression; but they are the way to victory and glory for Jesus her divine Son, "so that at the name of Jesus every knee should bend of those in heaven, on earth, and under the earth, and every tongue should confess that the Lord Jesus Christ is in the glory of God the Father" (Phil. 2:10 f.). The thought of these mysteries filled the mind of Mary and kept her heart aflame with holy love, sustaining her devotion.

Men are superficial, given to externals, earthly-minded. Therefore there is so much love of the world, so little appreciation of the beauties and joys of the spirit. Mary, the Singular Vessel of devotion, surely presents a needed lesson and shows the way to true devotion in the service of God.

## SPIRITUAL JOY

Devotion in the service of God and the spirit of prayer are productive of interior joy, even in the midst of sorrow and suffering. Sorrow may afflict the servant of God, but it does not reach the bottom of the soul; the storm may rage all around, but it does not penetrate into the depths of the heart; there is peace, the sense of security, because the servant sees himself in the hands of a loving God, who knows how to direct all things well. Therefore St. Paul rejoices in the midst of all his tribulations and exhorts the faithful to rejoice in the Lord. He knows whom he has believed. But if St. Paul, and with him innumerable saints, could thus rejoice in their sorrows, must not the Blessed Virgin have done so in an immeasurably higher degree, since more than all the other saints she loved God, possessed the spirit of prayer, and, having given herself over completely to the service of God, felt safe in the hands of His providence?

Spiritual joy can and must be fostered, since it plays such an important part in the Christian life. Not only does it lessen the weight of the cross, but it renders the practice of virtue so much easier and cheerful and thus also more meritorious. Sunshine must prevail in life; then darkness, rain, and snow will also speed the growth in holiness. After the pattern of our Blessed Mother we can become vessels of devotion, from which arise the sweet aroma of all-embracing self-oblation to our Creator and Father in heaven.

# Mystical Rose

FLOWERS belong to the most beautiful things of our visible creation. They seem to be remnants of Paradise, to carry so little of the curse that rests on this earth in consequence of man's transgression. The very word conjures up before our minds sunshine and blue skies, jeweled meadows and blooming gardens, fragrant breezes and sprouting life. No wonder men love flowers and use them as signs of their joy and hope, as symbols of virtues. Christians will always associate flowers with the heavenly paradise and see the saints as flowers blooming there eternally. The queen of flowers is the rose; so we are not surprised that the Queen of all saints is likened to the rose. She is called the Mystic Rose, the rose that encloses mysteries within itself. We discover mysteries in her origin, in her unfolding and blooming on earth, in her heavenly transfiguration. As the Mystic Rose she blooms forever in the heavenly paradise, a delight for God and all the angels and saints.

ORIGIN

The end and purpose of all creation, "the firstborn of every creature," as St. Paul puts it, is Jesus Christ, the God-man. "All things have been created through Him and unto Him" (Col. 1:16), because in Him creation was to find its crown and consummation. To counteract the destruction threatened by sin, divine Wisdom also decreed from all eternity, "to re-establish all things in Christ, both those in heaven and those on earth" (Eph. 1:10). In those eternal decrees Mary stands next to Christ as His Mother. Therefore holy Church applies to her the words, "The Lord possessed me in the beginning of his ways, before he made anything from the beginning" (Prov. 8:22). The Mystical Rose has its roots in the depth of the Godhead, in the eternal decrees of our salvation. Is it not significant that right after the Fall, amid the bloom and fragrance of Paradise, mention is made of her who would be the Mystical Rose as the woman who should crush the serpent's head? Even while one Paradise is being lost, another one is in preparation, and in it shall bloom forever living flowers, more beautiful than all the flowers of the first Paradise; their Queen shall be the Mystic Rose.

## Unfolding of the Rose

In the stillness of the morning, under the rays of the rising sun and the moisture of heavenly dew, the rosebud slowly opens; one by one its tender petals unfold until it shines in all its queenly beauty. So heaven's Mystic Rose began to stir and sprout in the holy ground of a chosen ancestry and holy home. The rays of the Holy Spirit's love awakened her to life in wondrous beauty: "Grace is poured abroad in thy lips; therefore God hath blessed thee forever. With thy comeliness and thy beauty set out, proceed prosperously, and reign" (Common Office of the Blessed Virgin). Like Jesus, Mary advanced in age and wisdom and grace before God and men. Faith deepens, hope grows stronger, the flames of love reach higher. Mary was the rose that the Holy Spirit would offer to the Son of the eternal Father on the day of His espousals with the human race, as the pattern of "the Church in all her glory" (Eph. 5:27).

## In Full Bloom

We behold the Mystic Rose in full bloom on the day of the Annunciation, when the Word was made flesh and dwelt among us. She blooms in the spotless white of purity, unworldliness, and piety during the Saviour's infancy and hidden life, "The brightness of eternal light and the unspotted mirror of God's majesty and the image of His goodness" (Mass of the Most Pure Heart of Mary). As years pass and the bloody glare of the Passion intensifies, white changes into crimson to match the bloody shades of Calvary. The sight of the Mystic Rose in her crimson glory was the sweetest comfort of the dying Saviour. At last red turns into bright triumphant gold in the glorious mysteries of her life. She who so faithfully shared in the labors and sufferings of His life now also shares in His glory of victory.

TRANSPLANTED

Earth could not be the lasting abode for beauty such as that of the Mystic Rose. The day came, when she was transplanted from this earth to the heavenly paradise, not only in soul, but also in body. Now the mysteries that were hidden in her shine out into the vast expanses of heaven to fill the angels and saints with reverence and wonder and delight for all eternity. White, red, and gold are the ground colors of this Mystic Rose, but they intermingle and form new combinations and patterns without number. Now the riches and beauty of Mary's virtues can be seen in their glory unveiled.

The beauty of the Mystic Rose is the inspiration of the saints. In fact, the saints are all her offspring; this is the unique distinction of the Mystic Rose, that she brings forth not only roses, but every flower that blooms in God's paradise, in the Church Militant and Triumphant. Just as flowers differ as to color, form, and fragrance, so the saints differ, but they all find in the Mystic Rose the pattern and inspiration of their holiness. Mary is the Mother of all saints of the past, of those who live in our days, and those who will live in times to come to the end of the world. And so with the appearance of the Mystical Rose, "the winter is now passed, the rain is over and gone, the flowers have appeared in our land" (Cant. 2:11). May we be among them!

# Tower of David

ANCIENT cities were surrounded by walls into which towers were built to serve as vantage points and armories in the defense of the city. The tower of David was the strongest tower in the wall of Jerusalem. When David had recaptured Mount Sion from the Jebusites, he built upon it a tower so strong that it should never again fall into the hands of the enemy. However, in the course of time the superstructure of this tower fell into ruin and only the foundation remained. King Herod built upon it three gigantic towers, the strongest of which was called the tower of David. It was so strong that it survived even the destruction of Jerusalem. When after the fall of the city the Roman general Titus inspected this tower he exclaimed, "Truly we have waged this war with the help of God. Human bravery and war machinery could not have taken this place." Against this historical background the meaning of the above title becomes clear. Mary is an impregnable tower of protection in the conflict with the powers of hell, and an armory in which all weapons needed for the Christian warfare are to be found.

## IMPREGNABLE FORTRESS

The Church of Christ on earth is the Church Militant, and the life of the Christian is a warfare. Although Jesus is the Prince of peace, He tells us that He has not come to bring peace, but the sword. He wants us to remember that His peace follows victorious warfare. So it was in the beginning and so it will be to the end of the world.

The warfare opened with Satan's attack in Paradise. It was an attack, not by physical force, but by deceit, and Satan, the father of lies, scored his first victory. God came to the rescue of our fallen race and gave us hope of eventually defeating the enemy and rising from the Fall. He said to the serpent, "I will put enmities between thee and the woman, and thy seed and her seed; she shall crush thy head and thou shalt lie in wait for her heel" (Gen. 3:15). This is a belligerent prophecy; it speaks of warfare, but also of victory. God Himself will build a wall of protection for men and the strongest point in that wall will be the Tower of David, David's greatest daughter and Mother of David's greatest Son. Before this impregnable Tower the advance of the enemy will be halted; here he will be defeated and his head crushed.

Mary's immaculate conception, her virginal motherhood, and bodily assumption into heaven are the high lights in Satan's defeat. Through Mary deliverance from the power of Satan has also come to us, but Satan will return to the attack; the conflict will continue until final victory is won through perseverance to death. Through Mary we shall be victorious.

## ARMORY

God, who built this impregnable Tower of David, also made it the armory for all weapons and war machinery the Christian people would need. As such Mary is described in her type, the spouse in the canticle, "Thy neck is as the tower of David, which is built with bulwarks; a thousand bucklers hang upon it, all the armor of valiant men" (Cant. 4:4). Mary is compared to the neck because, as the neck connects the head with the body, so Mary connects Christ the Head with His mystical body, the Church. From this Tower of David the Christian takes his armor and weapons for the Christian warfare. What this armor and the weapons are St. Paul tells us: "Stand therefore having girded your loins with truth, and having put on the breastplate of justice, and having your feet shod with the readiness of the gospel of peace, in all taking up the shield of faith, with which you may be able to quench all the fiery darts of the most wicked one. And take unto you the helmet of salvation and the sword of the spirit, that is, the word of God" (Eph. 6:13 ff.). Of this word of God the same Apostle says, "The word of God is living and efficient and keener than any two-edged sword, and extending even to the division of soul and spirit, of joints and marrow, and a discerner of the thoughts and intentions of the heart" (Hebr. 4:12). This word of God comes out of the mouth of the incarnate Word of God, the Son of her who is the Tower of David (Apoc. 1:16). The weapons are all spiritual because, "our wrestling is not against flesh and blood, but against the principalities and powers, against the world rulers of this darkness, against the spiritual forces of wickedness on high" (Eph. 6:11).

Mary not only supplies these weapons but she also shows by her example how to use them. She was true to God, just in all her ways, filled with love of God and men, unwavering in her faith and hope; she wielded the sword of the spirit as no other Christian warfarer can wield it by giving us the eternal Word of the Father in the form of man.

There is profound comfort in this title for our days, which are clearly approaching the most dreadful onslaughts of the powers of darkness. The fury of hell is increasing; the weapons employed betray diabolical cunning, resourcefulness, and cruelty; the strategy is one of astounding adaptibility to conditions and opportunities. We need the comforting assurance that God and His saints are with us. This title offers this assurance. Mary is with us, and where she is there is also her divine Son. Mary, who at Fatima played with the sun as a child plays with a ball, what will she not do, when the decisive moment arrives! From the Tower of David will sally forth the legions of Mary to crush the enemies of God. David's greatest Son has built this Tower, and the gates of hell shall not prevail against it.

# Tower of Ivory

IVORY was a highly prized commodity in ancient times. Rich people would use it for beautifying their homes; in some of these ivory was so prominent that they were called ivory houses. Ivory houses and palaces therefore became associated with the idea of wealth, refinement, joyous feasting. The title Tower of ivory thus quite naturally follows the preceding one: Tower of David. In the latter the idea of war and all its hardships dominates, whereas Tower of ivory suggests the idea of peace and joy, the fruit of victorious warfare. The height of a tower, the qualities of ivory, the social inferences suggested by ivory buildings all point to some characteristic excellence in the person of our Blessed Mother.

## HEIGHT

Towers as a rule rise above surrounding buildings and afford a free and unobstructed view of all the scenery around. Mary, towering above all angels and saints by the grandeur of her mission and holiness, affords a wonderful outlook upon this world, as far as the human race reaches in space and time. In her we behold the eternal decrees of divine wisdom and love unfolding. In the fullness of time, "The angel of the Lord declared unto Mary and she conceived of the Holy Spirit; and the Word was made flesh," and took up His abode in this ivory Tower. In due time He stepped forth from this abode to do the work assigned to Him by the Father and to die for the salvation of the world. And while He offers Himself upon the cross as the Victim for the atonement of sin, sacrifice is also offered in this Tower of ivory: Mary offering Him and all her love and her mother's rights to the Father. So it had been decreed that a woman should co-operate in man's salvation, as a woman had co-operated in the ruin of the human race. A glorious view indeed, overpowering in its grandeur.

## BEAUTY AND STRENGTH

The creamy white, the faultless luster of ivory when polished, must make an ivory tower beautiful to see. Mary reflects the splendor of the Beauty ever ancient, ever new. To the beauty of the material is added the beauty of the structure. The Holy Spirit Himself is the Architect of this Tower and He employed infinite wisdom and love in its building. If we compare saints to towers, and the comparison is justified, we notice that deficiencies of form and proportion are found in them. No saint is free from all imperfections. There are saints who excel in one virtue and are rather ordinary in other virtues, saints who excel by their desire for a certain virtue rather than by its perfect practice. In Mary everything is perfect, every virtue present in that degree of perfection that is proportionate to its importance; there is no flaw, no excess, no defect. All fair art thou, O Mary.

Ivory is extremely hard and resists the ravages of time and climate and weather to a degree that almost equals that of the hardest metals. So does Mary, the Tower of ivory, stand before us in unchanging splendor. She does not experience the deteriorating effects of fickleness and discouragement; good and evil days find her the same; joy does not make her overbearing; sorrow does not evoke complaint. She is always the humble handmaid of the Lord, whose delight is to do the will of God.

## WEALTH

Ivory towers because of their costliness could be built and appropriately furnished only by the wealthy. The Tower of which we speak was built by the infinitely rich God, and He has bestowed upon it wealth and splendor such as only God can bestow. St. Paul gives thanks to God, "for the grace of God, which was given you in Christ Jesus, because in everything you have been enriched by him" (1 Cor. 1:4). The riches of spiritual gifts received by the faithful allow conclusions as to the spiritual wealth bestowed upon the Mother of Christ. What could God withhold from her to whom He had given Himself as Son? As God has stored up in Mary, the Tower of David, all the armor and the weapons needed for the Christian warfare, so He had hidden in her, the Tower of ivory, the unfathomable riches of Christ for the benefit of all who love Him and His holy Mother.

## Joy

Psalm 44 pictures the bride of the Messias-King as awaiting the bridegroom in an ivory palace, from which the sound of stringed instruments welcomes Him. So did the sound of music and heavenly jubilation welcome the Messias-King as He entered this Tower of ivory to assume the form of man. Never ceasing songs of love and adoration resounded in Mary's heart during those nine months when the incarnate Word of God dwelt in her. In that Tower of ivory originated the *Magnificat,* which ever since has sent its sweet melody over the face of the earth and will resound through the heavens for all eternity. We must dwell in this Tower and there ponder over the divine mysteries wrought in it, in order to experience more and more of the joy of Mary's heart. In and with the joyful Mother of God, "Come, let us praise the Lord; let us joyfully sing to God our Saviour" (Ps. 94:1).

Men built the tower of Babel in their proud desire to reach the heavens and to perpetuate their greatness. They did not succeed; God confused their language, so that they no longer understood one another and had to separate. God built the Tower of ivory in His Blessed Mother, and this Tower truly reaches into heaven, perpetuating the wonderful dignity of human nature and uniting all men in brotherly love. Beauty, riches, power, security, peace, and joy are found in this Tower. Let us turn these thoughts into prayer when we say: Tower of ivory, pray for us.

# House of Gold

IN THE year 64 Rome was destroyed by fire. In rebuilding the city Emperor Nero had a magnificent palace built for himself. Within the palace walls and ceilings were overlaid with gold and set with jewels. The ceiling of the banquet hall was made of ivory tiles, some of which were movable so that through the openings flowers could be dropped on the guests; others were supplied with tiny tubes to spray the hall with perfumes. When Nero entered this palace for the first time he was delighted and exclaimed, "Now at last I dwell like a man." This palace was called the golden house. Its magnificence suggests thoughts and comparisons for the better understanding of the title given to Mary: House of gold. When the human race had been ruined by the terrible conflagration of sin, the eternal Son of God, King of the universe and Redeemer of the human race, built for Himself a house of gold in which He would dwell. And when for the first time He entered it as the God-man He could exclaim, "Now at last I dwell like God." Mary the Mother of Christ is this House of gold.

GOLD

Gold represents to us the highest value. Therefore gold was extensively used in temples and palaces. When Solomon built the magnificent Temple of Jerusalem, "there was nothing in the Temple that was not covered with gold; the whole altar of the

oracle he covered also with gold. . . . And he overlaid the cherubim with gold. . . . And the floor of the house he also overlaid
with gold within and without" (3 Kings 6:22 ff.). St. John in
the Apocalypse sees the heavenly Jerusalem built of pure gold;
even the street was of pure gold, as it were transparent glass.
Holy Church accepts this appraisal of the value of gold by
demanding it in the vessels for the celebration of the sacred
mysteries and the preservation of the Blessed Eucharist.

God Himself followed the same principle in building and
furnishing the house that was to be the dwelling place of His
eternal Son. However, it was not material gold which He used,
for even this has no value when compared to the gifts of His
grace and love. Gold is the symbol of love. God's love went
into the building of that house, the love of Father, Son, and
Holy Spirit. There is no grace or virtue that was not bestowed
upon Mary in the highest degree of perfection. God is love
and love is fire and the fire of that divine love enkindled in the
heart of Mary love strong as death, love that would give all to
God and retain nothing for herself. Gold is tested and refined
through fire; the gold of Mary's love was tested and brought
ever closer to the infinite purity of divine love in the tribulations
of her life. The seven sorrows of her life pierce her heart like
seven swords, but her "Love is strong as death. . . . Many
waters cannot quench charity, neither can the floods drown it"
(Cant. 8:6).

## Grace and Blessing

Mary is the House of gold, because the gold of divine love
and grace is there dispensed for the asking. When Solomon had
finished the Temple and dedicated it amid unparalleled festiv-
ities, God took possession of it. His presence filled the Temple
with a cloud, and He appeared to Solomon assuring him that
He had accepted this house as His own, that it would be a

house of prayer, and that He would hear the prayers of all those who would pray in this place. The Temple was the type of the churches of the New Testament and the promise of God applies especially to them. Holy Church assures us of this truth in the Communion verse of the Mass for the dedication of a church, "My house shall be called a house of prayer, saith the Lord; every one that asks therein receives; and he who seeks finds; and to him who knocks it shall be opened."

But Mary is the prototype of temple and church; she is the living abode of the Most High. The Blessed Eucharist, the life and glory of a Catholic church, had its first beginning in Mary, for in her was formed the body and the blood of the Saviour, who is truly and substantially present in the Blessed Sacrament. And in the first offering of the sacrifice of our salvation Mary as Coredemptrix stood beneath the cross of her dying Son. Therefore it is the will of God that all blessings of redemption should come to us through Mary. She is the House filled with the gold of divine blessings and desires most eagerly that we would avail ourselves of them. Therefore, like her divine Son, she is always making intercession for us, and every prayer united with that of Mary is sure to find a favorable answer.

The Christian must be a house of gold, because he too is the dwelling place of God. But he lives in the world and the greed of the world for material gold is in striking contrast to man's indifference to the gold of divine love and grace. We all may easily become infected by this spirit of the world. Yet gold has value only when it helps to express our love of God and becomes the symbol of love and sacrifice. The gold of true and genuine love, tested and refined in the furnace of tribulation, must be the ambition of the Christian, and he will find it in Mary, the House of gold.

# Ark of the Covenant

ON MOUNT SINAI God gave the Israelites the Ten Commandments and entered with them a solemn covenant. He reminded them that He had brought them out of Egypt to be His peculiar possession, a priestly nation and a holy kingdom. As in the past, so in the future, He would guide and protect them, if they would observe His commandments. The people answered as with one voice, "All that the Lord hath spoken we will do" (Exod. 19:18).

## COVENANT AND ARK

To keep the people mindful of His providence and faithful to their promises God commanded Moses to build the tabernacle, where the daily worship and the evident manifestations of God's presence would serve both purposes. The sanctuary, as it might be called, of the tabernacle was the holy of holies, in which was kept the ark of the covenant; the latter was a chest, made of the almost incorruptible wood of the acacia tree and overlaid with gold on every side. "In the ark was a golden pot containing the manna, and the rod of Aaron which had budded, and the tablets of the covenant; and above it were the cherubim of glory overshadowing the mercy seat" (Hebr. 9:4). Because it contained the three principal tokens of God's covenant with the people, it was called ark of the covenant.

The tablets of the law reminded the people of their obligation to keep the commandments. The vessel with manna could not but fill them with confidence and love of God, who had taken such wonderful care of them during their years in the desert. The rod of Aaron impressed upon them respect and obedience to their priestly leaders. God Himself had chosen Aaron and his tribe to perform the sacred functions of divine worship. And it was upon the mercy seat, that is, the cover of the ark, over-shadowed by the cherubim, that God manifested His presence ever so often in a visible manner and gave Moses instructions for the guidance of the people. This ark was the type of Mary, the Ark of the new covenant.

### Type Fulfilled

All the typical features contained in the ark find their fulfill-ment in Mary. The incorruptibility of the wood of the ark points to the absence in Mary of all corruption of sin and death. The gold used for the adornment of the ark typifies the richness of the endowments of Mary in body and soul.

Through her divine motherhood Mary becomes the depositary of the proofs of God's eternal love for men and His unchangeable will that all should be saved. She bears within herself not the tablets of the law but the Lawgiver Himself. The body and the blood which Mary gave to her divine Son, in the course of time become the true bread of life, the antitype of the manna. When Jesus promised the institution of the Blessed Eucharist He said, "I am the bread of life. Your fathers ate the manna in the desert and have died. . . . I am the living bread that has come down from heaven. If any one eat of this bread, he shall live forever; and the bread which I will give you is my flesh for the life of the world" (Jn. 6:48 f.). And Jesus, who is the bread of life, is also the "Priest forever according to the order of Melchi-sedech," chosen by the Father from all eternity; He is the anti-type of the priesthood of Aaron.

What the ark of the covenant was for Israel, Mary is in an immeasurably higher degree for the Christian people. Through her the presence of God among men assumes a new, astounding form, enters most intimately into the life of the individual Christian. God not only manifests His presence in some miraculous manner, but He becomes man Himself, dwells among men, speaks with them, helps and heals them, offers the great sacrifice of man's salvation on the cross and perpetuates it in the eucharistic sacrifice, the memorial of all His wonderful works. Thus Mary is linked to the history of the Christian people from the beginning unto the consummation of the world. It is then that she will be seen in all her glory as the Ark of the New and Everlasting Testament, bearing witness that all promises of God were fulfilled. "And the temple of God in heaven was opened and there was seen the Ark of his covenant in his temple" (Apoc. 11:19).

## THE CHRISTIAN AN ARK OF COVENANT

The glories of Mary as the Ark of the Covenant are also ours in a true, though modified, sense. God has entered a covenant with us in baptism. He gave us His commandments; we promised to keep them and He in turn promised us life everlasting. In Holy Communion we receive the true manna that has come down from heaven and, incorporated into Christ, we become "a chosen race, a royal priesthood, a holy nation, a purchased people" (1 Pet. 2:9). As such we offer not only spiritual sacrifices but, according to Pius XII, we participate even in the offering of the eucharistic sacrifice, "in a twofold sense, namely, because they (the faithful) not only offer the sacrifice through the hands of the priest, but also to a certain extent in union with him."

The way in which the Israelites acted toward the ark of the covenant was decisive for their condition as a nation and as individuals. Loyal service and worship of God was followed by blessings; defection from the covenant brought upon them severe punishments, which eventually led to the loss of the ark and the rejection of the people. So will the state of the faithful, as nations and as individuals, depend upon their attitude toward Mary. "Through Mary to Jesus" is a universally accepted principle. True devotion to Mary cannot but lead to the loyal keeping of the covenant with God, to love of Jesus in His eucharistic mystery, to a profounder understanding of the priestly, sacrificial element in the Christian life. Indifference to or rejection of Mary, on the other hand, will lead to indifference in faith, rejection of Christ, and to all the other dreadful consequences of godlessness.

# Gate of Heaven

THE patriarch Jacob, fleeing before his brother Esau to Mesopotamia, one night had a dream vision. He saw a ladder reaching from earth to heaven, God at the top and angels ascending and descending. At the same time he heard the voice of God promising that in one of his descendants all the tribes of the earth would be blessed. When Jacob awoke in the morning he was overawed and said, "Indeed, the Lord is in this place and I knew it not. How terrible is this place! This is no other but the house of God and the gate of heaven" (Gen. 28:16 f.). The vision came to fulfillment through Mary, the Mother of Jesus, in whom all the nations were blessed. In her liturgy holy Church gives us what we might call a commentary on this title of our Blessed Mother, who truly is the gate of heaven. In the Lauds of the Office of the Blessed Virgin she is called the Gate of the great King; in the Vespers, the Blessed Gate of heaven; in the Marian antiphon of Advent, the Open Gate of heaven; and in that of Lent, the Gate from which light has risen for the world.

## GATE OF THE GREAT KING

In the Nicean Creed we profess that Jesus came down from heaven for us and our salvation. He could have come in the maturity of manhood as Adam came forth from the hands of God; He could have come in countless other ways, which would not have necessitated the co-operation of any created agency. However, He chose to enter this world as a child, through human though miraculous birth: conceived of the Holy Spirit, born of a virgin.

Jesus is the great King. Great, because He is King of the universe, and His kingdom is spiritual and everlasting. His Mother, through whom He came into the world, is therefore the Gate of the great King. So sublime is the majesty of this King that the Gate through which He enters must be reserved for Him alone. He is the only Son of Mary as He is the only Son of His eternal Father; Mary is virgin before, in, and after the birth of Christ. The words of the prophet Ezechiel are meant for her: "This gate shall be shut, it shall not be opened, and no man shall pass through it, because the Lord, the God of Israel, hath entered in by it, and it shall be shut for the prince" (Ezech. 44:2).

## BLESSED GATE OF HEAVEN

Mary is the chosen Gate, filled with happiness and joy. Gabriel, the archangel sent by God, and Elizabeth, filled with the Holy Spirit, call her blessed among all women. There must be blessedness supreme in her, who could call the Son of the eternal Father her Son, and give to the world the long-desired

Saviour. Blessed is she in the possession of the God of joy, who had given Himself to her with completeness and abundance as to no other human being. The Spouse in the canticle rejoices because, "I found him, whom my soul loveth; I held him and I will not let him go" (Cant. 3:4). Mary has found the God of her heart. He is her Son and she is His Mother, and this relationship of Son and Mother can never be changed. Not only does she hold fast to Him, but with an infinitely stronger hold does He keep her to Himself. Blessed is she in the perfect conformity of her will with the will of God, which to do was her daily meat, as it was the daily meat of her divine Son. Blessed is she in the consciousness of having been chosen to co-operate with God in the salvation of the world. The climax of this blessedness shall come on the last day, when she shall behold the uncounted numbers of the redeemed entering the kingdom of the Father, in which Her Son shall rule forever. She was the Gate through which the blessed came to know and love and serve Jesus and thus be saved.

GATE OF LIGHT

During the Lenten season, the days of salvation and the acceptable time, the days of penance and purification, holy Church sings, "Hail thou gate, from which light has risen to the world." The Gate of heaven must be a gate of light, since heaven is the place where God dwells in inaccessible light, where the Lamb, the Son of Mary, is the Lamp. Through Mary, as it were through a gate, streams of heavenly light fall upon this earth. Things appear in the color of the light that falls upon them, red or green or blue; they appear to us in something like heavenly transfiguration when light from heaven falls upon them. How insignificant then appear work and labor, when compared with the reward they earn; humiliations, how comforting they are, when seen in the heavenly exaltation which they merit; sufferings and persecutions, how sweet and desirable, when viewed in the light of eternal victory, refreshment, light, and peace. Jesus did not exaggerate when in the eighth beatitude He said, "Blessed are you when men reproach you and persecute you and, speaking falsely, say all manner of evil against you for my sake. Rejoice and exult, because your reward is great in heaven" (Mt. 5:11). It was a glorious sunrise for the world when Jesus, the Sun of justice, rose through this Gate of light and let streams of heavenly light fall upon the world.

This beautiful title is but another version of the old Catholic saying: Through Mary to Jesus. Christ the great King has come to us through Mary; through Mary He will rule over hearts and nations. Peace, joy, and happiness, which the world cannot give but for which the human heart is craving, are streaming through this Gate; let us avail ourselves of them. From this Gate is heard in heavenly, motherly accents the invitation, "Come, eat my bread and drink the wine which I have mingled for you" (Prov. 9:5). This gate is ever open. No eye has seen, no ear has heard, no human heart has experienced what lies beyond it. That some day we may see and hear and experience we address to Mary, the Gate of heaven, the lines of a popular hymn:

> "Through thee may we enter the haven of rest
> And worship forever in courts of the blessed."

# Morning Star

WITH all the night life of modern times people have lost appreciation of the beauty of the starry sky. The fascination of artificial light has blinded them to the awesome glory which the Giver of all light has displayed in the firmament. "The heavens show forth the glory of God and the firmament declareth the work of his hands" (Ps. 18:2). It was different in ancient times when there was less artificial light and men were more dependent upon the stars. The Christian mind soon discovered in some of the stars apt illustrations of the Blessed Mother of God. Thus she came to be called Morning Star, Star of the sea. The title Morning Star suggests some striking comparisons.

REFLECTED LIGHT

The morning star, like the earth, is one of the planets in our solar system; it does not shine by its own light but reflects the light of the sun. So is the Blessed Virgin of herself devoid of light and beauty, being a creature like the rest of men. Whatever she has, she has received from God. If she outshines all the stars in the firmament of saints, it is because the light of God's glory falls upon her in greater abundance: "Every good gift and every perfect gift is from above, coming down from the Father of lights" (James 1:17). Her divine Son is the Sun of justice; must we not expect that He will bestow upon her a beauty and brilliance that will mark her at once as the chosen one of God? And the absence of any dark spot of sin or sinful attachment renders possible a faultless reflection of the divine light.

REVOLVING AROUND THE SUN

The morning star revolves around the sun; the sun is the determining factor of its movement and orbit. So Mary's life revolves around the divine Sun; God — after the Annunciation, more concretely, the incarnate Word of God — is the determining factor of her life and activity. There is not a thought in her that does not ultimately terminate in God, no desire that does not unite her with God more intimately, no word that does not promote His glory, no deed that is not performed in loving conformity with the divine will. As the morning star revolves around the sun with physical necessity, so Mary's life revolves around her God and Son with the force of love stronger than the force of any law of nature.

## HERALD OF THE DAY OF REDEMPTION

The morning star, the last star visible in the sky before the rising of the sun, is the herald of the dawning day. How welcome morning is after a night of suffering and loneliness; pain and sorrow are felt more keenly during the night than during the day.

The night of paganism covered the larger part of the earth before the coming of Christ. The empire of death was universal; the prince of darkness ruled supreme. No wonder that good and God-fearing men longed and prayed for the coming of a Redeemer, and that the glory of the Messianic times as described by the prophets aroused in them a burning desire for the coming of the day of redemption.

Mary, as the Morning Star of this day of redemption, stood in the sky of the Old Testament — the Woman that would crush the serpent's head, the Virgin that would conceive and bear a Son, whose name would be Emmanuel. At last there came the dawn of the day of redemption. The rays of the rising sun penetrated into the little town of Nazareth, and the Word was made flesh. And when the divine Sun rose above the horizon at Bethlehem, night was changed into day. The day of redemption had come and it will last to the end of time. We walk in its light and enjoy its blessings.

## HERALD OF THE DAY OF ETERNITY

The day of redemption is but the preparation for the day

of eternity, and Mary, the Morning Star of the former, is also the Morning Star of the latter. In the splendor of her bodily assumption Mary proclaims the glory and the delights of this eternal day. Beyond the portals of death begins another life, another world, in which the faithful servant of God receives his wages, the victorious soldier his crown. There is the home of the family of God, there the kingdom of all the redeemed over which Christ shall reign forever. "Oh, how glorious is the kingdom, wherein all the saints rejoice with Christ; they are clothed in white robes; they follow the Lamb whithersoever it goes" (Feast of All Saints, antiphon for *Magnificat*).

The day of eternity is the perfect day; perfect in the absence of any and every thing that might mar its beauty or disturb its harmony; perfect in the possession of all that the heart can desire; perfect in its endless duration. Death shall be no more, nor mourning, nor crying, nor sorrow; no heat or burden of the day, no hunger and thirst, no strife or struggle; the blessed shall drink from the fountains of life and be inebriated with the plenty of the house of God. God Himself shall be their reward exceedingly great. What beautiful vistas are opened up for us by the Morning Star of the eternal day, vistas of that "incorruptible inheritance, undefiled, and unfading."

We need the guiding and cheering light of this Morning Star in the apocalyptic darkness and confusion of our days. In its light we recognize the true meaning of life as a preparation for eternity. After the example of Mary, the Christian life must reflect the light of divine truth; it must be God-centered, taking the will of God as the determining factor of thoughts and words, intentions and deeds. And as the end of life approaches we will turn our eyes to the eternal horizons and there we shall behold Mary as the Morning Star, gently calling us to come and rest and taste forever the peace and joy of the eternal day.

# Health of the Sick

GOD created man in perfect health and bestowed upon him, besides, the gift of bodily immortality. There would have been neither sickness nor death in Paradise; both are the punishment of sin. Notwithstanding the atonement made for sin by our Saviour's Passion, sickness and other bodily suffering will remain the lot of men to the end of time; impassibility and immortality are reserved for the life to come. But in our suffering there are with us Jesus, the divine Physician, and His holy Mother, the Health of the sick, ever ready to help. Where health of the body would not be for the best of the soul, grace can and will open our eyes to the merit and glory of suffering and strengthen us to accept it from the hand of God as a gift of His love. In the present invocation we implore such help from our Blessed Mother.

## HEALING OF THE BODY

Even though the mission of Christ was principally spiritual, it did not exclude the alleviation of bodily suffering. St. Matthew writes, "And Jesus was going about all Galilee, teaching in their synagogues and preaching the gospel of the kingdom and healing every disease and every sickness among the people" (Mt. 4:23). Not only did Jesus Himself heal the sick, but He bestowed the power of healing also upon the disciples when He sent them out on their first missionary journey, and He

113

perpetuated this power when He gave the Apostles His last
missionary command: "They shall lay hands upon the sick
and they shall get well" (Mk. 16:18). Even many of the faithful
received this power; the charism of healing was of rather common occurrence in the ancient Church. Miraculous healing
through the intercession of the saints has never died out in
the Church; the miracles, mostly healings of the sick, that
precede the frequent beatifications and canonizations in our
times are evident proof of it.

It might seem strange that neither in Scripture nor in Tradi-
tion do we find any record of Mary having healed the sick
during her earthly life. However, not all things said or done
have been recorded, not even in the case of Christ, and, subject
to the judgment of the Church, we may piously supply what is
wanting. If Apostles and saints could lay their hands upon the
sick and heal them, should we deny that something similar
happened when the loving and compassionate Mother of Jesus
met with suffering people imploring her help? Could her
motherly heart resist the appeal of their suffering, the tears and
prayers of their friends and relatives? As centuries move on,
Mary's power is revealed with ever increasing impressiveness.
No other saint has wrought more numerous or more conspicuous
healings of the sick than the Blessed Mother of Jesus. Her
shrines, scattered throughout the world, give testimony of her
power and love.

HEALING OF THE SOUL

All bodily suffering in the last analysis is a punishment of
sin, which is the disease of the soul. Health in the full sense
of the word comprises well-being of body and soul. Therefore
Mary as the Health of the sick will invariably turn her attention
to the soul of the sick. She will direct the thoughts of the
sufferer to the blessings of suffering and thus strengthen him

to accept his cross as a proof of divine love. Indeed, God strikes in this life in order to save in the next. It is this thought that inspired the prayer of St. Augustine, "O Lord, here strike, here cut, here burn, but spare me in eternity."

Suffering atones for sin. The justice of God demands punishment of sin in this life or in the next. Yet the sufferings of this time are insignificant when compared to the sufferings of the next life. The thought, then, that we can pay off the debt of our punishment in an immeasurably easier way is a consideration which to a believing Christian must afford profound comfort and alleviation.

Suffering is a protection. To a great extent it makes the enjoyment of worldly pleasures impossible and in a general way subdues the craving of nature for such pleasures. It opens the eyes to the vanity, transitoriness, and deception of worldly pleasures and fixes the gaze on heaven, where alone true joys are found.

Suffering brings home to us with irresistible evidence our weakness and dependence upon God. All medical skill and all the will power of the sick man cannot make him well and preserve him from death, when the hour appointed for him has come. God controls the destinies of man and we must submit to His will or suffer for all eternity.

Patient, loving suffering is meritorious and shares in the merit and glory of the Passion of Christ: "If we have died with him, we shall also live with him; if we endure, we shall also reign with him" (2 Tim. 2:12).

Next to Jesus no one ever suffered as did Mary His Mother. She suffered in her soul what Jesus suffered in the body. The Queen of all martyrs understands the meaning of suffering; she has experienced its pain and sorrow, but also its glorious blessings. Therefore she is qualified to be and, in fact, is the Health of the sick. Her motherly heart goes out to all poor

sufferers to restore them to health and bring them relief, if
not for the body, then for the soul. All suffering patiently and
lovingly borne in union with her and her divine Son will
merit for the sufferer eternal well-being for soul and body in
heavenly glory.

# Refuge of Sinners

MUCH more deserving of pity and in need of help than
those sick of body are the sinners. They are sick in soul when
in venial sin; they are spiritually dead when in mortal sin.
Moreover, sin, especially habitual mortal sin, has left the soul
in a state of general weakness, accompanied by an increase in
power of inordinate passions. Whereas in bodily sickness men
often have remedies to relieve or remove suffering, there is no
natural remedy for the alleviation or removal of sin. However,
we are not left without hope and help. The present invocation
directs our attention to Mary as the Refuge of sinners. The
sinner can do nothing better than entrust his case to her; to
help and to save sinners is her delight as it was the delight of
Jesus who had come to call sinners to repentance and to seek
the lost sheep.

## THE MIND OF JESUS

If ever two hearts beat in unison, they are the hearts of Jesus
and Mary. If therefore we want to know the attitude of Mary
toward sinners, we must first know the attitude of Jesus. The
evangelists have given us a moving portrait of Jesus in His
love and quest of sinners. He seeks sinners wherever they are:

in cities and villages, on streets and in public places. He follows them, mingles with them, eats with them, shows them so much kindness that the Pharisees are scandalized and murmur, "This man welcomes sinners and eats with them" (Lk. 15:2). Jesus answers His critics with the parables of the lost sheep and the lost drachma, and concludes, "I say to you that even so there will be joy in heaven over one sinner who repents, more than over ninety-nine just who have no need of penance" (Lk. 15:7). No sin, no matter how grievous or repulsive to the Heart of Jesus, is excluded from His love and forgiving mercy. He saves the adulterous woman from condemnation, defends the sinful woman who came to anoint His feet, has a look of tender pity for Peter who denied Him, and the promise of paradise for the repentant thief.

## THE MIND OF MARY

The mind of Jesus is also the mind of Mary. Could Jesus' love for sinners, so deep and tender, leave the heart of Mary unaffected? What must we expect of the most loving Mother of men, of the Virgin merciful? The desire of Jesus for the salvation of sinners fills her heart, she shares in His grief and sorrow over unrepentant sinners. The joy of Jesus over finding the lost sheep is also the joy of His Mother. But let us see this mind of Mary more in detail.

Mary's profound knowledge of the justice and holiness of God gives her a penetrating vision of the malice of sin, which is a rebellion against the almighty God, a provocation of His justice. The mere thought of sin is unbearable to her sinless heart, the commission of a sin so revolting a sight that she turns away from it in horror. Spiritual shortsightedness and blindness are the reason why the sinner does not see the abysmal deformity and ugliness of his act. Mary sees, and her innermost being urges her to bring to an end such a dreadful state.

The Blessed Mother loves Jesus as no other human heart ever loved Him; His interests are her interests. She feels that every sin is a profound disappointment of His love. Unrepentant sinners render in vain the shedding of Jesus' precious Blood and make forgiveness impossible, "since they crucify again for themselves the Son of God and make him a mockery" (Hebr. 6:6). Mary's motherly impulse to save Jesus from such sorrow and disappointment and to glorify His mercy cannot but urge her with irresistible force to love and seek the salvation of souls for whom Jesus shed His blood.

Lastly, the Mother of the Saviour is fully aware of the office assigned to her in the economy of our salvation as the new Eve and the spiritual Mother of men. It is the thought stressed by Pius XII: "As another Eve she offered Him on Golgotha to the eternal Father for all the children of Adam, sin-stained by his fall, and her mother's rights and mother's love were included in the holocaust. Thus she, who was corporally the Mother of our Head, through the added title of pain and glory became spiritually the Mother of all His members" (*Mystici Corporis*). Dangers beset the paths of men, Satan and the evil spirits are prowling about the world seeking the ruin of souls, the world holds out all her attractions to weak human hearts. Could Mary, the Mother of men, be indifferent, seeing her children snatched away by Satan and dragged down to eternal perdition?

Truly, it has never been heard that anyone was ever foresaken who placed his confidence in Mary the Refuge of sinners, performed some little act of devotion in her honor, and did not completely reject her help. The most hardened sinners have returned to God when Mary's help was sought. It was the experience of St. Clement Hofbauer that he never failed to arouse a dying sinner to repentance, if he had time to say the rosary on his way to the dying. The prayer addressed to Mary daily by millions of men will not go unheard: Holy Mary, Mother of God, pray for us sinners now and at the hour of our death.

Two thoughts suggest themselves at the end of these reflections: never to lose courage because of our own sins and never to despair of the conversion of a sinner, no matter how obdurate he may be. Mary is the Refuge of all sinners. Let us take to her loving and motherly heart all our sins and infidelities, all our regrets and sorrows, all our fears and anxieties because of sins committed in the past. In Mary, the Refuge of sinners, we will find mercy, peace, and joy in the Lord.

# Comforter of the Afflicted

NOT without reason is this earth called the valley of tears, and it is significant that this is done in the prayer we address to our heavenly Mother: the *Salve Regina*. If all the tears ever shed on earth were gathered, they would fill an ocean. Sorrow affects a man more keenly than bodily suffering, it cuts into his very soul; it is felt all the more deeply if the afflicted is alone with no one to share his grief. Sorrow will never completely disappear from this earth, but it can be made sorrow unto life and not unto death. An element of joy and love can be injected even into the most bitter grief of soul, and then suffering becomes the royal road to holiness and heaven. To give this happy turn to our afflictions is what we ask of Mary, the Comforter of the afflicted. She knows the causes of sorrow, she disposes of the sources of consolation, and she loves us.

### CAUSES OF SORROW

The causes of sorrow are well nigh innumerable; they may be within us, they may come from without. Past sins and the violence of temptations may be prolific sources of sorrow; loneliness may afflict the heart, failure in work may bring keen disappointment, conditions of life may seem unbearable. We do not have the things we need, the things we would like to have. We are kept in a place for which we do not care, must do work which we loathe; uncharitableness and injustice may rob us of all trust in our fellow men and embitter our hearts. But to yield to discouragement or despondency would make matters only worse.

Mary was free from sorrows and regrets caused by personal sin and moral weakness, but there were other sorrows that filled her heart to overflowing. Throughout her life, even during the peaceful days of Nazareth, Calvary with all its terrors loomed before her, since she knew the prophecies concerning the Saviour's Passion and death. Recall her loneliness and fear when Jesus was lost in the Temple, her grief at the sight of the indifference of men toward God and divine things, their earthly-mindedness, their ingratitude toward her divine Son. All this must have been a continuous torture for her heart burning with love of God and men. Yet, in a much more penetrating and sublime manner than the Apostle, she was, though sorrowful, yet always rejoicing and abounding with consolation in the midst of all her tribulations.

### SOURCES OF CONSOLATION

The source of all true consolation in whatever affliction is God, "the Father of mercies and the God of all comfort" (2 Cor. 1:3). But we must turn to Him through faith and hope and love.

There can be no more solid consolation than the unwavering

faith that God governs the world and that nothing can happen against His will. If He allows sorrow to afflict us, He does so because it is for our good: "Now we know that for those who love God all things work together unto good" (Rom. 8:28). Moreover, "God is faithful and will not permit you to be tempted beyond your strength, but with the temptation will also give you a way out, that you may be able to bear it" (1 Cor. 10:13).

Hope lifts up from the depths of sorrow and points to the glorious heights to which affliction borne for Christ will lead us. "Did not the Christ have to suffer these things before entering into His glory?" Sorrow will not last forever, death will put an end to it. Life is short, so the end of sorrow cannot be far away. Beyond the gloom and darkness shines the sun of eternal peace. "For our present light affliction, which is for the moment, prepares for us an eternal weight of glory that is beyond all measure; while we look, not at the things that are seen, but at the things that are not seen. For the things that are seen are temporal, but the things that are not seen are eternal" (2 Cor. 4:17 f.).

Love sees grand opportunities in affliction, which is the food of the saints, as St. Gregory the Great says. Saints are formed in the school of suffering; the world will be redeemed only through the cross. The blessings of redemption will be brought to sinners and to those outside the Church not only through preaching and prayer, but also and especially through the vicarious sufferings of Christ-loving souls. So much suffering in the world is lost and even turned into poison; sorrow permeated by love is the crying need of the hour; to be able to supply that need by patient and loving endurance of tribulations and thus to fill the hunger of the Heart of Jesus for souls must be a source of profoundest comfort in affliction.

St. John beheld the great multitude of the saints in heaven, "clothed in white garments with palms in their hands," and received the information that, "these are they who have come out of the great tribulation, and have washed their robes and made them white in the blood of the Lamb" (Apoc. 7:14). All the saints carried the cross of their tribulations in their earthly lives. At their head stands the Blessed Mother of Jesus. To what extent these saints owed their loving endurance to Mary, the Comforter of the afflicted, will be fully seen only in eternity. But all the saints, together with their Queen, drew their joy and consolation from faith and hope and love.

If we would rejoice in afflictions and make them sources of blessing, we must seek the consolation offered by Jesus through His holy Mother. Worldly consolations work like narcotics, causing temporary relief but soon changing to misery and distress. They are nothing but the vanity and vexation of the spirit of which the wise man speaks. Blessed are they who mourn in the company of Jesus and Mary, for they shall be comforted — by the Comforter of the afflicted.

# Help of Christians

IN THE three preceding titles we have considered the help which our Blessed Mother brings to the faithful in their private needs: health to the sick, hope to sinners, comfort to the afflicted. In the present invocation we consider Mary as the Help of Christians, that is, of the faithful as members of the Church Militant. It is through perversion of the truth, corruption of morals, and persecution that Satan and his legions operate against the Church; against these dangers we implore the help of Mary.

## Perversion of Truth

It is significant that heresies, which are nothing but perversions of the truth, arose in the Church from the very beginning, even during the lifetime of the Apostles. It is related that St. John met one of the earliest heretics, Cerinthus, on a public street, and when asked by Cerinthus whether he knew him, the Apostle answered, "I know you, the first-born of Satan." There is hardly a doctrine of the faith that has not been attacked in the course of time: the mystery of the Blessed Trinity, the divinity of Christ, the virginal motherhood of Mary, grace, the mystery of the Blessed Eucharist, the infallibility of the Church. But in all these errors the heretics themselves still kept faith in God and in unchanging principles of morality. Modern times have reached the nadir of possible errors by denying the very existence of God and of any definite and eternal principles of truth; according to some moderns there is no absolute truth, and what we call truth is nothing but temporary social agreement serving temporary interests.

In these perversions of the truth Satan is at work, and he does here exactly what he did in Paradise. He deceives, urging men not to believe the word of God, but to find out for themselves; to judge according to their own principles and thus to assert their liberty. Satan has much cause for satisfaction with the results accomplished in the confusion of religious and moral ideas. Millions of men have been robbed of faith in God and the existence of anything supernatural or spiritual and, left to their own judgment, have drifted ever farther away from the truth, and from the justice and love of a common human brotherhood under the Fatherhood of God.

In the Office of the Immaculate Conception it is said of Mary that she alone has overcome all heresies. This she has done not by any spectacular interference with the course of events but by her very person, office, and endowments. She *is* the Virgin Mother of the Saviour and the spiritual Mother of all men, and remains for members of the Church a unifying factor against all separatist tendencies of heretics and other perverters of the truth.

## Corruption of Morals

The members of the Church are not immune to sin and vice. St. Paul already had reason to complain, "For many walk of whom I have told you often and now tell you even weeping, that they are enemies of the cross of Christ. Their end is ruin, their god is their belly, their glory is in their shame, they mind the things of earth" (Phil. 3:18). The severe penitential discipline of the early Church allows some conclusions as to the moral conditions of the faithful in those times. Corruption of morals had much to do with the revolt against the Church in the sixteenth century. In the seventeenth century, devotion to the Sacred Heart was the means chosen by our Lord Himself to arouse the faithful to greater fervor, against the coldness and indifference of so many, even of souls consecrated to Him in the religious and priestly state. And does not our Lady of Fatima complain of the growing wickedness of the world and point to prayer and penance as the remedy? If such conditions are found among the faithful, we cannot expect them to be better in the world at large.

The Blessed Virgin is the Help of Christians in this need. It has become strikingly apparent that whenever devotion to the Blessed Mother increased, betterment of morals also set in. In fact, we witness such a change for the better as the result of the growing popularity of the rosary devotion. The faithful, who are one in their love and devotion to the Mother, are also one in the love of her divine Son and in obedience to His law.

PERSECUTION

Persecution was never completely absent from the Church, but in our days we are witnessing an intensification of it in forms more cruel and inhuman than were ever known in history. The future will reveal, at least in part, the number of martyrs and confessors who have suffered and died for the faith even in our day.

The seriousness of the situation must turn our attention to Mary, Help of Christians. She has proved her power again and again in the defense of Christianity. The decisive battle of Lepanto, 1571, in which the Moslem fleet was destroyed, was fought on the first Sunday of October, while in Rome the members of the rosary confraternity held their customary processions. Soldiers in that battle carried the rosary around their neck and the flag of the commander in chief displayed the image of the Blessed Mother with the Infant Jesus on her arm. Again in 1683, the Moslems had advanced as far as Vienna and had been besieging the city for several months, when Christian forces under the command of the Polish King Sobieski arrived. The battle cry of the Christian soldiers was "Jesus and Mary," as they stormed to the attack. The Moslem army was completely routed and Vienna set free. In gratitude to the Blessed Mother for her help on that day Innocent XI instituted the Feast of the Holy Name of Mary, celebrated annually on the twelfth of September.

There is hope also for our times that through the help of the Mother of God the forces of communism will be defeated. In that stupendous sun miracle of Fatima we have received the pledge of Mary's power and her promise that Russia will be converted, if the faithful take up the arms of prayer and penance. All the while, even behind the iron curtain, the image of the Blessed Mother, so dear to the Russian people, is venerated and the light of hope burns in millions of hearts. As in the past so in the future Mary will prove herself to be the Help of Christians.

# Queen of Angels

THAT the Mother of the King of Angels should be Queen of Angels is a postulate of sound reason enlightened by faith. To which of the angels did the eternal Son say: "You are My Mother"? To which of the angels did the incarnate Word of God render obedience? Where is the angel that entered so actively into the economy of men's salvation as to become Coredemptrix and Mediatrix of all graces? The angels are "ministering spirits sent for service, for the sake of those who shall inherit salvation" (Hebr. 1:14). Mary is the Mother and Mistress of all the saved.

## EMINENCE OF OFFICE

St. Gregory the Great has this to say in reference to the offices assigned to the angels: "Angels are messengers, Archangels the most prominent class among these messenger angels, Virtues perform signs and wonders, Powers restrain the demons, Principalities preside over angels, Dominations exercise authority over them, Thrones assist at the divine judgments, Cherubim excel by the depth of their knowledge, Seraphim are said to be burning or set on fire because of their flaming love" (Breviary, Common of Angels). If we use this interpretation for an evaluation of the tasks assigned to the Blessed Mother of God, we get a more definite picture of Mary's queenly eminence over the angels. Mary receives the most important message ever sent to this world and an archangel, whose very name points to the importance of the message, delivers it: Gabriel, the Power of God. Mary is the object of the message given by angels to the shepherds during Christmas night: she is the Virgin Mother, who had wrapped the divine Infant in swaddling clothes and laid Him in a manger. All signs and wonders ever wrought by angels are eclipsed by the sign of which Isaias speaks, "Behold a virgin shall conceive and bear a Son, and his name shall be called Emmanuel" (Isa. 7:14). This Virgin Mother and her Child shall break the power of the demons forever. As Mother she exercises authority over the God-man; if her wish is command for the Son of the eternal Father, what will it be for even the mightiest angel! Should not the Virgin Mother, who was so intimately associated with the divine mysteries of our salvation, have of them a knowledge surpassing that of the Cherubim? Must not she, through whom has appeared the love of God that set the world on fire, burn with more than seraphic love?

## Victorious Over Evil Spirits

When Lucifer raised the cry of rebellion in heaven, Michael and his followers rose in defense of the honor of God. "And there was a battle in heaven; Michael and his angels battled with the dragon and the dragon fought and his angels. And they did not prevail, neither was their place any more found in heaven. And that great dragon was cast down, the ancient serpent, he who is called devil and Satan, who leads astray the whole world; and he was cast down to the earth and with him his angels were cast down" (Apoc. 12:7 f.). The test which led to the rebellion of the bad angels is believed to have been the adoration of the incarnate Word of God, shown to them in vision. May we not assume that in this vision they also beheld the Mother of the eternal Son of God? If so, it was then and there that the good angels, eager to behold and adore the God-man, also offered their love and loyalty to their future

Leader and Queen. She would have a leading part in the defeat of Satan's kingdom on earth, for she it is of whom God spoke when He said to the serpent, "I will put enmities between thee and the woman, and thy seed and her seed; she shall crush thy head . . ." (Gen. 3:15). The holy angels delight at the prospect of final and glorious victory and pledge their faithful allegiance as long as the warfare shall last, as long as there will be evil spirits prowling about the world and seeking the ruin of souls.

## SERVANTS AND MESSENGERS

Holy Scripture speaks of angels as ministering spirits. They appear as leaders and defenders of the chosen people, protectors of the Temple, the executors of divine judgments. They are the guardians of men, who inspire good thoughts and in every way possible endeavor to bring us closer to God. The services which Mary has rendered and is rendering to God and men are more sublime and have brought to the world more blessing than the services of all angels combined. She has given to the world the Saviour, and in our spiritual regeneration and the development of our supernatural life she acts the part of our spiritual Mother; both services are fundamental and essential to our salvation and a life of holiness.

A particular service rendered by the angels to men is implied in their name: they are messengers. So Gabriel was sent to the prophet Daniel foretelling the time of the Saviour's coming; the same archangel was sent to Zachary to announce to him the birth of the precursor, and a short time after this to Mary with the grandest message ever sent to this earth. It was a message that brought heaven down and changed the course of history. The mere reception of such a message through such a messenger would mark the Blessed Virgin as the Queen of all angelic messengers. However, the Blessed Mother of God is herself the most queenly messenger of God. She does not proclaim her message in words, but she gives to the world the incarnate Word of God, who is the Truth, the Way, and the Life. Her own life and office is a message. Her immaculate conception, virginal motherhood, and glorious assumption into heaven proclaim the infinite wisdom, power, and love of God. She is the great sign blazing forth the great message of God's condescension and man's exaltation, a message so grand and beautiful, so inspiring and elevating, as to exceed the boldest dreams or expectation of any created mind.

Let us lift up our eyes and behold her entering into heaven and all the choirs of holy angels gathering around her to pay their homage and jubilantly to proclaim her as their Queen.

# Queen of Patriarchs

AMONG the saints in heaven we count as the first in the order of time the patriarchs, the ancestors of the human race and in particular of the chosen people. In speaking of Mary as the Queen of Patriarchs we will confine ourselves to the most prominent among them: Adam, Noe, Abraham, and Jacob. If she stands in queenly majesty above these four, she does so even more with regard to all the others. Typical events in the lives of these patriarchs find their fulfillment in and through Mary and set in striking relief this title of her glorious queenship.

### ADAM

Having created our first parents God placed them in the Paradise of pleasure; so happy was their life that to the present

day we associate it with supreme happiness. The happiness of
Paradise did not last long. However, sin did not put a stop to
the love of God. Another Man and another Woman will undo
the harm wrought by their ancestors and inaugurate a second
creation more glorious than the first. Mary, Adam's greatest
daughter, is this Woman. Adam is the father of a fallen race,
deprived of the glory of divine life and sonship. Mary is the
Mother of the Saviour, Giver of divine life, who restored the
dignity of human nature to a state more wonderful than it was
in the beginning. And through her divine motherhood she becomes the Mother of a spiritual race, a new progeny, "a heavenly offspring, conceived in holiness and born again as a new
creature" (blessing of baptismal water).

## Noe

The human race in its vast majority followed in the path of
the rebellion of their first parents. "And God seeing that the
wickedness of men was great on the earth . . . it repented Him
that He had made man. . . . He said: "I will destroy man, whom
I have created, from the face of the earth" (Gen. 6:5). Amid
the general corruption Noe and his family alone were found
to be just, and therefore saved from destruction by means of
the ark. After the Deluge Noe left the ark and offered to God
a sacrifice of thanksgiving. It was then that God established a
covenant with Noe and his posterity, and promised that the
human race would never again be destroyed by a flood. The
typical events in Noe's life point to the eminence of Mary
over Noe.

Noe was a just man; Mary was just in an immeasurably
higher degree. Noe was saved from physical destruction; Mary
was saved from the deluge of sin in her immaculate conception.
God enters a covenant with Noe and his descendants; through
Mary the eternal Son of God establishes the new and everlasting

covenant with mankind. Not only were men never to be destroyed by water, but "by the mysterious power of one and the same element an end was to be put to sin and a beginning given to holiness" (blessing of baptismal water). Noe's sacrifice of thanksgiving is surpassed infinitely by the sacrifice of Mary's Son; as far as in her lay, she offered Him with all her mother's rights and love. The mysterious character of this sacrifice allows that it be offered up not only once, but daily to the end of time, as the perpetual sacrifice of thanksgiving.

## ABRAHAM

Abraham was chosen by a special divine call to be the ancestor of the chosen people. Since Abraham was justified by faith and not by the works of the law, he likewise became the spiritual ancestor of the chosen people of the New Testament. Thus we speak of him as "our father Abraham" in holy Mass. The typical features in the life of this patriarch add new claims to Mary's queenship among the patriarchs.

Abraham's call is surpassed by the call of Mary to be the Mother of the Saviour and spiritual Mother of all the redeemed. Abraham becomes the father of Isaac through a special intervention of divine power; Mary becomes the virginal Mother of Christ through the overshadowing of the Holy Spirit. Through Isaac, Abraham was to become the father of a great nation, and in one of his descendants all the nations of the earth would be blessed. Mary is the Mother of this greatest descendant of Abraham, and through Him all nations received the blessing of eternal salvation. Abraham was great in his faith and obedience. Notwithstanding the anguish of his father's heart and the apparent contradiction in God's procedure, he reasoned, "that God has power to raise up even from the dead" (Hebr. 11:19). His faith was rewarded; Isaac was saved from death the very moment Abraham lifted up the knife for the fatal blow. Mary with immeasurably greater faith and love offered her divine Son, and though she saw Him die, believed that He would rise again. And she did see him alive in immortal glory, and in due time her own self raised to the same glory through her glorious assumption. This is incomparably more than all the virtues and distinctions of "our father Abraham."

JACOB

The history of Jacob abounds with typical facts pointing to Mary as Queen of Patriarchs. There is the dream vision of the ladder reaching from earth to heaven, granted to the holy patriarch. It is fulfilled in and through Mary. Gabriel descends, bringing to Mary the message of her election; he returns, taking with him the Virgin's answer: she is the handmaid of the Lord. Then the Son of the eternal Father descends as Son of Mary, and in due time returns to the Father, not alone, but bringing with Him the souls of Limbo and later the saints of all ages in an unbroken line. To the end of time this constant intercommunication between God and men goes on: angels taking up to heaven the prayers and good works of men, and God sending down from heaven the blessings of redemption. Would Jacob ever have thought of such a fulfillment of His vision?

Jacob endured the agonizing pain of believing that his favorite son had been killed by a wild beast, when the treachery of his brothers sold Joseph into Egypt. But he also experienced the joy of seeing him alive, invested with royal dignity and acclaimed by the Egyptians as saviour of the world. Mary not only believed her Son dead, but saw Him die on the cross, abandoned and betrayed by His people; she also saw Him alive, King of the universe, Saviour of the whole world.

Jacob is the father of twelve sons, who become the ancestors of the twelve tribes of Israel. Mary is the spiritual Mother of the twelve Apostles, and these again are the spiritual ancestors of the faithful of all generations from all tribes and tongues and nations.

When the dying Jacob blessed His son Juda, he prophesied that the scepter would not be taken away from Juda until the Desired of the nations would come. The Desired of the nations came: the Lion of Juda, the Son of David. He is the Son of Mary. His kingdom, though in the world, is not of the world; it is a spiritual kingdom, the Church Militant, that will pass over in due time into the Church Triumphant, where He shall reign in the house of Jacob, and of His kingdom there shall be no end.

Mary is the Mother of the immortal King of ages, towering mountain high above all the saints of the heavenly kingdom — the patriarchs' most glorious descendant and now their heavenly Queen forever.

# Queen of Prophets

ALL prophecies concerning Christ are in a certain sense also prophecies about His Mother. When Isaias speaks of the Child that is born to us, the Son that has been given to us, we must think also of the Mother of that Child. If Bethlehem is not the least among the towns of Juda because from it will come forth the Leader of the people, would Bethlehem be that town without His Mother? The infancy of the coming Messias is unthinkable without a Mother taking care of Him. Not only in this indirect way, but also directly and explicitly, do prophets speak of Mary. Let us recall three of them.

## PROPHECIES IN PARTICULAR

At the head of all prophets stands Isaias, the Evangelist of the Old Testament, as he is called. He speaks of Mary's virginal motherhood as the great sign that would be given to the house of David, notwithstanding the wickedness of the then reigning king: "Hear ye, therefore, O house of David. . . . Behold a virgin shall conceive and bear a son, and his name shall be called Emmanuel" (Isa. 7:14).

There is Jeremias speaking of the restoration of Israel and the new covenant, "The Lord hath created a new thing upon the earth: a woman shall compass a man" (Jer. 31:22). The God-man had the use of reason from the very first moment of the creation of His soul, and therefore is spoken of as a man.

In Ezechiel's great prophecy the Blessed Mother appears as the sanctuary, the gate of which is closed except for the entrance and exit of the Prince: "This gate shall be shut, it shall not be opened, and no man shall pass through it, because the Lord, the God of Israel, hath entered by it, and it shall be shut for the Prince" (Ezech. 44:2).

## GLORY OF FULFILLMENT

Jesus Himself called the attention of the Apostles to their great privilege of associating with Him and witnessing the unfolding of the divine plan of redemption: "Blessed are the eyes that see what you see. For I say to you, many prophets and kings have desired to see what you see and have not seen it, and to hear what you hear and have not heard it" (Lk. 10:23). The prophets had seen the glories of the Messias from afar, obscurely, and in part; the Apostles beheld the wonderful reality. But no Apostle saw more or more clearly than the Blessed Mother of Jesus, who saw and heard and kept all these things in her heart, pondering over them and penetrating ever more deeply into the depths of these mysteries.

Vision of things to come made her a prophetess even before the Saviour had been born, before the Apostles had been chosen, when she sang her inspired *Magnificat*. All nations shall call her blessed because of the great things which the Almighty has done to her. She sees the mercy of God at work from generation to generation, His power that scatters the proud, puts down the mighty from their thrones, and exalts the lowly; in spirit she beholds God's fatherly goodness that fills the hungry with good things and sends the rich away empty; all happens just as He has spoken to the fathers. Is not all this incomparably more than what the prophets saw and announced? She is their Queen.

## Holiness of Life

The word of God must be announced by holy lips. The prophet Isaias tells of his own mystical purification in connection with his call to the prophetic office: "And one of the Seraphim flew to me, and in his hands was a live coal which he had taken with the tongs from the altar. And he touched my mouth and said, 'Behold, this hath touched thy lips, and thy iniquities shall be taken away and thy sins shall be cleansed'" (Isa. 6:6). We must say that on the whole the prophets distinguished themselves by the purity of their lives, their courage and zeal, their sufferings in behalf of the cause of God.

Mary surpasses the prophets in all these respects. Her purity of mind and heart is not the effect of a process of purification, since there was nothing in her to be purified; she was all pure and there was not a stain on her soul. Her advance in perfection is not the result of a more or less difficult struggle against inordinate inclinations, but the spontaneous and steady growth of a flower, the swift and majestic rise of the eagle into higher regions, the increasing splendor of the sun as it travels to the zenith. Hers is a life of uninterrupted prayer, a life of burning and consuming zeal, undisturbed tranquillity of heart, accomplishing infinitely more than all the prophets. All this prepared her for the everlasting vision of the Godhead face to face, and in her bodily assumption into heaven she is the first to enjoy the fullness of all the things the prophets foretold. Her very heavenly glory is a prophecy regarding our condition in life everlasting. She is herself the Queen of all prophets.

Prophecies are meant for us. They strengthen our faith, enliven our hope, and arouse a holy fervor in the certain expectation of the glorious things to come. The darker the prospects of the present from the human point of view, the more we need the light of prophecy to illumine the end of time and assure us of the final victory of the cause of God. "And we have the word of prophecy, surer still, to which you do well to attend, as to a lamp shining in a dark place, until the day dawns and the morning star rises in your hearts" (2 Pet. 1:19). May Mary, the Queen of Prophets, lead us to the place where, together with her, we shall admire and adore the wisdom and love of God, who from all eternity knows and ordains the things that happen in time, and behold the final, eternal, glorious fulfillment of all prophecy.

# Queen of Apostles

THE liturgy of the Church has beautiful things to say about the Apostles. They were friends of God, the chosen princes of God's people, sons born to God in place of the ancient patriarchs and prophets; their voice went out into the whole world, and together with Christ they shall sit on thrones to judge the twelve tribes of Israel. Yet, whatever may be the honors and prerogatives of the Apostles, Mary is their Queen.

## VOCATION

The Apostles were the first priests and bishops of the New Testament. Now, St. Paul tells us that, "No man takes the honor to himself; he takes it who is called by God as Aaron was called" (Hebr. 5:4). The very name of "apostle" designates one that has been sent. The Apostles were the heralds of Christ the King, sent to teach and baptize all nations and to make them disciples of Jesus. It is for the King and for Him alone to choose and send His messengers and representatives.

St. John records how Jesus called the first disciples to His following. In the course of time the other disciples were gathered, and when the appointed hour had arrived, Jesus, after having spent the whole night in prayer, called the disciples together, and out of them He selected the twelve Apostles. And Jesus wants the Apostles ever to remember that they had been called by Him. On the eve of His Passion He reminds them of it: "You have not chosen me, but I have chosen you, and have appointed you that you should go and bear fruit, and that your fruit should remain" (Jn. 15:16).

Mary's mission was more sublime than that of the Apostles; she too needed the divine call. We find it foreshadowed in many places of the Old Testament, which now holy Church applies to Mary in her liturgy, as for instance, "The Lord possessed me in the beginning of his ways, before he made anything from the beginning." Again, "Then the Creator of all things commanded and said to me; and he that made me rested in my tabernacle." The Annunciation was the completion of this eternal vocation. Mary understood and never needed to be

reminded of the fact that the Almighty had done great things
to her.

## HOLINESS

With the exception of Judas the Apostles were good and
holy men, though not without faults and failings. They were
culpably slow in grasping the teaching and spirit of the Master,
and for this they were reproached by Jesus; we find them given
to petty ambitions and jealousies and the desire for revenge.
During the Passion all, with the exception of John, abandoned
Him, and Peter even denied Him. It was only through a slow
process of formation in the school of the divine Master, and
then through the Pentecostal grace of the Holy Spirit, that
they were changed into the saints we know them to be now.
Totally different is the case of the Blessed Mother of Jesus.

We have often considered Mary's holiness; now we might
mention some of the virtues in which the Apostles distinguished
themselves. There is the deep and strong faith of Peter in the
divinity of Christ; he sees in Jesus the Son of the living God.
Paul is the most zealous Apostle with a heart as big as the
world, having but one ambition: that Christ be known and
loved throughout the world, and that he might spend himself
in His service. St. Andrew is the great lover of the cross, St.
John the loving and beloved Apostle of Jesus. But Mary is
Queen of them all. Her faith has brought us the God-man and
adored Him as an Infant in the manger; her zeal gave us
the Light and Life of the world; her love made her give up
her divine Son to the cruel death on the cross, that the world
might live by Him, even though this meant for her agony of
soul, more bitter than a thousand deaths.

## GLORY ETERNAL

It was at the Last Supper, in that heart to heart talk which

Jesus had with the Apostles, that He assured them: "You are they who have continued with me in my trials. And now I appoint to you a kingdom, even as the Father has appointed to me, that you may eat and drink at my table in the kingdom; and you shall sit upon thrones, judging the twelve tribes of Israel" (Lk. 22:28). As the Apostles were associated with Jesus in His life and work, so they will be associated with Him in His glory. They have made men disciples of Christ, fashioned the lives of men after the pattern of Christ, and it will be their never ending joy and glory to see that pattern in the glory of the saints.

More than any Apostle the Mother of Jesus continued with Him in His trials. And was it not Mary's task to form the image of Christ in her spiritual children? But the image of Christ is her own image, and she now beholds her own beauty and loveliness in the beauty and perfection of all the saints. She was and is their Pattern and Queen, if not known as such in their earthy lives, then so much the more admired, loved, and acclaimed as their Queen in everlasting glory.

The apostolic vocation is perpetuated by priests and religious and all those who dedicate their lives to the extension of Christ's kingdom on earth; the faithful must co-operate in the labors of these apostolic men and women. It is evident then that recourse must be had to Mary, the Queen of Apostles, in the present alarming shortage of apostolic vocations. She can and will show us the grandeur of the apostolic life, enlarge the hearts of the faithful to see beyond the boundaries of family, parish, and diocese the fields ripe for the harvest, fill them with generous love that is willing to offer not only encouragement and material support, but also personal service, so that soon there may be but one flock and one shepherd.

# Queen of Martyrs

MARTYRS are those holy men and women who have sealed their faith in Christ with their blood. Manifold are the ways in which they were put to death; they were scourged, crucified, stoned, pierced with arrows, thrown into seething oil, burned, devoured by wild beasts, beheaded, drowned, hanged, starved, buried alive, poisoned, shot. The Blessed Virgin suffered none of these things, she died in an ecstasy of love, surrounded by friends. Nevertheless she is the Queen of Martyrs by the intensity of her love causing lifelong mental martyrdom, and by the manner in which she suffered.

## LOVE

The essential element in martyrdom is the motive and not the endurance of death as such. A martyr is one who willingly and without defending himself suffers for the love of God in the practice of some Christian virtue. Intense pain capable of causing death may be felt not only in bodily torture, but also in compassionate love at the sight of suffering.

Mary surpasses all the saints by the intensity of her love. As she was full of grace, so she was full of love; it was in consequence of this love that the sufferings of Jesus truly became her own. She suffered with Him in His agony, the scourging and crowning with thorns, His crucifixion. Her suffering was so intense that it would have caused her death, had it not been supported by divine assistance. So she is dying again and again while she remains alive; the sword of sorrow daily pierces her heart; her suffering is long and deep and wide like the ocean that would have swallowed up her life a thousand times.

That Mary suffered more than all the martyrs together also follows from the place she holds in the economy of our salvation as Coredemptrix and Mediatrix of all graces. What the prophet says of Jesus also holds for Mary, though only in a secondary manner and by way of participation: "Surely he hath borne our infirmities and carried our sorrows . . . he was wounded for our iniquities, he was bruised for our sins; the chastisement of our peace was upon him and by his bruises we are healed" (Isa. 53:4 f.). All sorrow and pain of body and soul that would ever come to men in consequence of sin is gathered in the loving Heart of our Saviour's Mother, that there it might be united with the atoning sufferings of her divine Son.

## DURATION OF MARY'S SUFFERING

Generally speaking the tortures of martyrs, at least in their final, deadly intensity, did not last long; apart from this they may have spent the greater part of their lives in health and free from pain. Mary's martyrdom was lifelong. It began with the awakening of her reason. She knew Scripture and the light of the Holy Spirit gave her understanding of the mystery of man's redemption, which was to be accomplished by the sufferings and death of the Redeemer. The picture painted by Isaias must have been often before her mind: "There is no beauty in him nor comeliness. . . . Despised and the most abject of men, a man of sorrow and acquainted with infirmity . . . and we have thought him as it were a leper and as one struck by God and afflicted. He shall be led as a sheep to the slaughter" (Isa. 53:2 f.). She knew the psalms and understood for whom those words of the psalmist were meant: "O God, my God, look upon me; why hast thou forsaken me? . . . I am a worm and no man, the reproach of men and the outcast of the people; all they that saw me laughed me to scorn. . . . They have dug my hands and my feet, they have numbered all my bones. . . . They have parted my garments among them and upon my vesture they have cast lots" (Ps. 21). What an amount of suffering, what a crushing burden of fear and agony is crowded into those thirty-three years of Mary's association with Jesus. The memory of these sufferings lingered on in her mind even after the joy of Easter and the Ascension to the end of her life. This is more than any martyr endured.

## MANNER OF SUFFERING

We read of extraordinary ways and means by which God comforted some holy martyrs. Their prison was illuminated by heavenly light, wild beasts would not touch them, fire did them no harm, water would not drown them. The experience of such divine assistance must have given these martyrs a sense of joy and courage, and made them more or less insensible to pain. We know nothing of the kind in the life of the Blessed Mother and have every reason to believe that such consolations were not granted to her. Her consolation is that she can suffer with her divine Son without consolation. With Jesus she can say, "I looked for one that would grieve together with me and there was none; I sought for one to comfort me and I found none" (Ps. 68:21 f.).

It would be wrong to assume that Mary's faithful friends, like St. John and the pious women, did not try to console her and that she did not derive some measure of comfort from their love and sympathy. However, the height and depth, the length and breadth of her sorrow are beyond human reach; human minds cannot fathom the intensity of her grief, no more than they can fathom the intensity of her love. She suffers with her divine Son in unapproachable, sublime loneliness, truly the Queen of Martyrs.

Martyr means witness; witnesses of Christ we all can and must be. There is no more convincing, more noble and unselfish way of being a witness of Christ than the generous and loving acceptance and endurance of the cross, in whatever form it may come to us. According to *The Imitation of Christ* the highest virtue, the perfection of holiness is to be found only in the cross. The cross is the badge of honor, and the Queen of Martyrs pins it on her children. Martyrs we must be, if not of blood, then of love.

# Queen of Confessors

THE Church honors as confessors those holy men who attained to sanctity not through martyrdom but through the practice of heroic virtue. If Mary is the Queen of these men, then she is so much the more the Queen of all lesser saints. It will be sufficient for our purpose to consider three virtues, common to all confessors, because of their fundamental significance for the whole spiritual life: love of prayer, detachment, and fidelity to duty.

## LOVE OF PRAYER

When speaking of prayer we usually think of oral prayer, mental prayer, or the spirit of prayer. The latter form is the most perfect, being the habitual, spontaneous turning of the soul to God in all conditions of life. Confessor saints were familiar with all these three forms of prayer, though not all in the same degree of perfection. However, we find in all of them a serious striving after the spirit of prayer. St. Peter Canisius would spend at least seven hours daily in prayer; St. Gemma Galgani would say a prayer every fifteen minutes; St. Francis of Assisi was all absorbed in his favorite ejaculation: My God and my All. St. Aloysius, ordered by his superiors not to think so much of God in the interest of his health, found it impossible to banish the thought of God from his mind. God would occur to him wherever he might be, whatever he might do. St. Alphonsus prayed constantly and had wonderful things to say about prayer, its necessity and blessing for the Christian life, in his book on prayer as the great means of perseverance. Without prayer there is no salvation, much less sanctity. Prayer unites with God, inflames divine love, transforms into God.

Mary's eminent sanctity postulates eminence in prayer; we could not think of her except united with God in loving thought. The spirit of prayer draws her to the Temple, prompts her to take the vow of virginity. And what must have been her prayer life when the incarnate Word of God dwelt beneath her heart and lived in her company during those blessed years of Nazareth. Her soul was the most lovely and most holy habitation of God on earth and her spirit of prayer the sanctuary lamp that never failed.

DETACHMENT

Detachment from earthly possessions, the spirit of poverty, is another striking feature in the lives of the saints. St. Francis of Assisi returned to his father even the coat he wore and espoused poverty as his lady. St. Aloysius abdicated his right of succession to the duchy of Castiglione and assured his brother Rudolph that he, Aloysius, was the happier man. Where conditions made such complete renunciation impossible or inadvisable, the saints distinguished themselves by their generosity in using their wealth for works of piety or charity. St. Charles sold a principality and distributed the price among the poor in one day; he did the same with a legacy of 20,000 ducats which he had received. Of ecclesiastical revenues, with which he had been richly endowed, he kept for himself only what was absolutely necessary and gave the rest to the poor. During the fatal epidemic at Milan he offered his household furniture to be used by the sick, even his own bed, and he himself slept on the floor.

The saints showed such detachment because of their deep insight into the nothingness and danger of worldly possessions, unless used for the purpose for which God has given them. They understood the word of Christ, "What does it profit a man if he gain the whole world, but suffer the loss of his own soul?" (Mt. 16:26). And that other word of the divine Master, "So, therefore, every one of you, who does not renounce all that he possesses cannot be my disciple" (Lk. 14:33). Should Mary, possessing the gift of knowledge in the highest degree, have had a less clear insight into the purpose and meaning of created things? Daily she beheld the example of Jesus, who, "being rich, became poor for your sakes, that by his poverty you might become rich" (2 Cor. 8:9). Mary was poor and did not have much to give up, but had she owned the whole world she would have joyfully given it up for God and souls.

## FIDELITY TO DUTY

Each state of life has its particular duties; as these states are willed by God so are the duties attached to them. Confessor saints are found in all states of life: priests and religious, kings and peasants, professional men and laborers, the married and unmarried. To some great and important duties are assigned that attract the attention of men, to others small and insignificant tasks that hardly ever strike the eye or call forth favorable comment. To Mary were assigned low and humble duties. She took care of the Infant Jesus, did the laundry, cooked the meals, cleaned the house, mended the clothes, met the customers of St. Joseph, acted as hostess for visiting friends. Small services, indeed, but transfigured by the spirit of faith and love. The Blessed Mother viewed all these things as ingredients in the work of redemption, and that was enough for her to give these duties all the attention and care of which she was capable. Thus she became the example of all saints, an example which they imitated but never could equal.

This title is of eminently practical significance for the faithful in the ordinary states of life. For all of them the way to holiness is prayer, detachment, and fidelity to duty. Prayer makes us live in the presence of God, detachment is inseparable from self-denial, fidelity to duty gives us the certainty of always doing the will of God. This is the way to Christian perfection, and this precisely should be the object of our petition when we call upon the Queen of Confessors to pray for us.

# Queen of Virgins

VIRGINITY holds a prominent place in the economy of our salvation as well as in the life of the Church. Under the first aspect we have considered virginity in the title: Holy Virgin of Virgins; in the present title we consider it in its significance for the members of the Church. We speak here not of factual virginity, which is of obligation for all unmarried persons, but of a freely chosen, consecrated life of virginity. Such virginal life is most excellent and meritorious, of profound significance for the individual and for the world at large. We see it in all its glory and inspiration in the life of the Queen of Virgins.

## PERFECT CONSECRATION

Even in the Old Testament God demanded of priests and Levites a special holiness and consecration, not indeed through a virginal life, but through outstanding fidelity in the observance of the law and abstinence from conjugal relations during their period of service in the Temple. Higher demands were made upon the ministers of God in the New Testament. The example of a virginal life is given by Christ Himself, His Blessed Mother, St. Joseph; it is imitated by some Apostles like St. John and St. Paul, and followed also by the other Apostles, who gave up their conjugal life after they had definitely joined the apostolate. The law of celibacy for priests of the Latin rite goes back to at least the fourth century; to some extent it is in force also in the Oriental Churches which are in communion with the Holy See. The idea underlying this law is that those, who represent the virgin High Priest Jesus Christ and daily offer the virginal Lamb of God upon the altar, should in their own lives present the ideal of priestly consecration and sacrifice, and that is done most impressively by a virginal life. As the ideals of Christianity took deeper roots among the faithful, many others, men and women, felt the desire of thus consecrating their lives to God; some, in fact the majority of them, would do so in the religious state, others would continue to live in the world. Even before knowing the ideals of the New Testament Mary had consecrated her life to God through the vow of virginity. She grasped the significance of a virginal life and all its implications to a degree that makes her the Queen of all virgins.

## SIGNIFICANCE FOR THE WORLD

Next to the instinct of self-preservation the instinct of race preservation is the strongest in human nature. In the state of original innocence it was under the perfect control of reason;

sin unleashed its uncanny power which it now exercises over human nature. Man, refusing to submit to the will of God, must now submit to the humiliating vexations of the flesh. Virginity faces the impure spirit courageously and deals him a decisive blow; it renounces even the lawful gratification of the sex instinct in married life, in order to live entirely for spiritual ideals. Once victory has been gained over the passions of the flesh, victory over all the other evil inclinations becomes much easier. This explains why we find in the virginal state the greatest number of saints. They stand before us as conquerors and heroes in the forefront of the Christian army. Mary, the Queen of Virgins, who has crushed the serpent's head, is the Leader of the glorious army of virgins that follow the Lamb wherever It goes.

The world can see in virginity the possibility of living a chaste life. If men are to rise from the morass of sensuality, they must have an ideal to look up to, something to hold on to. In its attempt to deny the possibility of a chaste life and to besmirch the character of those who have chosen it, the world reveals its very esteem and admiration for it and admits its own weakness and cowardice.

## To Foster and Preserve Virginity

Not all are called to the virginal life: "Not all can accept this teaching, but those to whom it has been given" (Mt. 19:11). However, it may also safely be said that many who receive this call do not accept it. For this reason the ideal of the virginal life must be fostered and, once it has been chosen, the means to preserve it must be employed. We find these means illustrated in the life of the Blessed Virgin: prayer and retirement, avoidance of worldly distractions and enjoyments, self-denial, charity, the desire to please God. Devotion to the Queen of Virgins, of course, should occupy the first place next to Christ.

Her protection is all-powerful and dreaded by the impure spirit. The very sound of her name stops the tempter from approaching; no one will turn to her with confidence without experiencing a gradual weakening of sensual desires and a growing love for the ideal of purity. St. Thomas says that the pure beauty of the Blessed Virgin awakened love of this virtue in all who looked at her. St. Jerome, writing against Helvidius, asserts that the sight of the Blessed Virgin strengthened St. Joseph in the love and practice of his virginal life. But, even though all the means are used, virginal life will, generally speaking, always be a life of uninterrupted conflicts with Satan, the world, and corrupt nature; virginal chastity can grow and flourish only on ground watered by the tears and blood of self-denial. However, the peace and joy it engenders in the soul, the blessings it brings to the world are worth the sacrifice, and the glory which it merits in the life to come is well described by the inspired writer as "singing a new canticle which no one else can sing, and following the Lamb whithersoever it goes."

We need the example and inspiration of the Queen of Virgins today more than ever. Though not all are called to the virginal life, all will find in Mary's example and intercession courage and strength for the observance of the chastity of their particular state of life. "O how beautiful is the chaste generation with glory . . . it triumpheth crowned forever, winning the reward of undefiled conflicts" (Wisd. 4:1 f.).

# Queen of All Saints

THE characteristic features in the holiness of Mary, that make her the Queen of All Saints, are its grandeur, detachment, service, universality, inspiration. Let us examine these features in the liturgical texts which holy Church applies to Mary.

## GRANDEUR

"I was exalted like a cedar in Libanus" (Ecclus. 24:17). The cedar is distinguished by its majestic height, the excellence of its wood which is almost incorruptible and highly polishable, so that it was used extensively for the building of temples and palaces. Mary towers above all saints. God chose her to be the palace and temple of the incarnate Word, and therefore made her incorruptible of soul through her immaculate conception and fullness of grace, and of body through her bodily assumption into heaven.

Such a towering height of holiness, though beyond our reach, is a challenge to aim high. With the help of grace and Mary's motherly assistance it is possible to keep the soul free from the corruption of deliberate sin, to increase the beauty and splendor of the temple, which the Holy Spirit has built in our souls; there is no limit to the heights of holiness that we may reach. Therefore: aim high — each day must bring you closer to God.

## DETACHMENT

"I was exalted like the palm in Cades" (Ecclus. 24:18). The palm, used for the comparison in this case, sheds its leaves as it grows; straight and slender it rises into space; only at the top it keeps the leaves necessary for growth, and there it produces flower and fruit. It is the symbol of victory that can be accomplished only through self-denial and detachment.

Mary, the Queen of All Saints, without any attachment to the world, rises straight to God; close to God she produces the flowers and fruits of her love. Detachment from this earth is needed, if we would give our minds and hearts to God, and in the higher sphere of divine light and love bring forth the fruit of holiness. Hence: be detached, conquer yourself.

## SERVICE

"As a fair olive tree in the plains" (Ecclus. 24:19). The olive tree was valued highly for its all-around usefulness. Its fruit provided light, nourishment, and healing.

Mary gave to the world Him who is the Light of men, the Bread of life, and the Remedy for all of mankind's ills, especially moral disease and suffering. Throughout her life she was most intimately united with her divine Son in placing all her words and deeds in the service of souls. Love of God and of our neighbor is the great commandment of the law. The Christian life by its very nature is therefore consecrated to service. Hence: make yourself fit for service, and remember that in no other way can you do more for God and souls than by a holy life.

## UNIVERSALITY

"As the vine I have brought forth a pleasant odor and my flowers are the fruits of honor and riches. I am the mother of fair love and of fear and of knowledge and of holy hope. In me is all grace of the way and of the truth, in me is all hope of life and of virtue" (Ecclus. 24:23 ff.). The vine is valued because of its fertility and the excellence of its fruit. Christ speaks of Himself as the vine and of us as His branches; He chose wine as the second element for the eucharistic sacrifice, the joy and hope of the world.

Christ, the Vine, is the fruit of Mary. If we are the branches of Christ, then we are also the branches of Mary. It remains for us to be living branches, bearing the fruits of love and fear and holy hope and of all virtues. The riches of this Vine are worth more than all the gold and silver and precious stones

found on the face of the earth. The fruit of the vine is changed
into the blood of the Saviour at the eucharistic sacrifice. It
is to this wine that St. Ignatius addresses the petition: "Blood
of Christ inebriate me." Should it not inebriate us with holy
love of God and forgetfulness of self, and keep us ever active
in producing all the fruits of a holy life?

INSPIRATION

"I gave a sweet smell like cinamon and aromatical balm; I
yielded a sweet odor like the best myrrh" (Ecclus. 24:20).
There is something pleasing and stimulating about these aro-
matic substances. So there is something refreshing and stimulating in a holy life. The sacred writings speak of the sweet odor
of good deeds, of sacrifice, of a holy life.

No saint has exercised on the members of the Church as great
an influence as the Mother of the Holy One. Particularly stimulating in her life is the fact that there is nothing which, according to the standards of the world, would be spectacular or
world-shaking. But we do find in her life the humble, lowly
things for which the world has no eye: humility, fidelity to
duty, kindness, sympathy, patience. Yet these her humble
virtues have done for the salvation of the world more than all
the spectacular deeds of statesmen, generals, scientists, and
artists. Spectacular deeds are beyond the possibility of the vast
majority of men, but the charm and drawing power, the world-
embracing and world-transforming power of deeds of holiness
are within the reach of all. Words teach, examples draw.

# Queen Conceived Without Original Sin

THE Council of Trent, dealing with the universality of original sin, declared expressly that it did not intend to include in this doctrine the Blessed Mother of God, thus implying that she is the only exception to this universal law, the only one conceived without original sin. Yielding to the insistent petitions of almost the whole Catholic world Pius IX, on December 8, 1854, solemnly defined, "The doctrine, which holds that the Blessed Virgin Mary was preserved from the state of original sin by the singular grace and privilege of the almighty God, in view of the merits of Christ, the Saviour of the human race, is revealed by God and therefore to be believed by all the faithful firmly and steadfastly."

## DOCTRINE

The meaning of this doctrine is not that Mary was sanctified before her birth as was St. John the Baptist, but that God created her soul in the state of sanctifying grace, and that thus she was never stained by original sin. God preserved Mary from original sin in view of the merits of Christ. Mary's immaculate conception therefore is not independent of Christ; she too has been redeemed by her divine Son, but in a more excellent manner than the rest of men. The grace of redemption was applied to her not after but in the very moment of the creation of her soul.

Holy Fathers and theologians see the immaculate conception foreshadowed in the burning bush, which Moses saw in the desert. The bush was burning yet not consumed by the fire. So Mary, although entering life in the same way as the rest of men, was not injured by the general conflagration of original sin.

The mystery is seen prefigured in the Ark of Noe, which was not swallowed up by the waters of the Deluge; so did the deluge of original sin do no harm to the Blessed Mother of God.

Another type of the immaculate conception is the ark of the covenant in its passage over the Jordan. When at the end of their wanderings through the desert the Israelites arrived at the Jordan, it was springtime and the water was high. But as soon as the Levites carrying the ark stepped into the river, the waters halted and rose up like a mountain to allow the ark of the covenant to be carried across. So the torrent of sin and corruption, carrying mankind down to the Dead Sea of perdition, stopped in its course to let Mary, the new Ark of the Covenant, pass untouched. The immaculate conception is Mary's exclusive privilege; no other human person has shared in it nor ever will.

### FITTINGNESS

There is divine wisdom and harmony in the eternal decrees of man's salvation. Mary had been chosen to be the Mother of the Saviour, Coredemptrix and Mediatrix of all graces. Could we imagine that such an exalted position in the work of redemption is compatible with the humiliation of having been under the influence of sin even for a moment? The angels were created in the splendor of immaculate purity; could we expect less for the Queen of Angels? Adam and Eve came forth from the hands of God in the state of grace; and the greatest of their daughters, she who was to undo through her divine Son the damage done by them, should be denied the glory of such sinlessness? Our Catholic sense rebels against such an assumption.

It would be an indignity to the Son of God, that He should take the flesh and blood of human nature from a Mother who had been contaminated by original sin; it is unthinkable that the Holy Spirit should choose for His Spouse one that had borne the mark of a slave of the evil spirit. There is incompatibility in the very idea that she, who was to crush the head of the serpent, should first have been stung by its poisonous fangs. It would be derogatory to the goodness of God to assume that He did not bestow upon Mary all graces and privileges that ever had been bestowed upon a created person. Precisely this thought is implied in the words of Pius IX: "God enriched her so wonderfully from the treasury of His divinity, far beyond all angels and saints with the abundance of all heavenly gifts, that she, always free from every stain of sin, all fair and beautiful, should show forth such fullness of innocence and holiness, than which a greater under God is unthinkable and which, beside God, no one can conceive even in thought."

LESSON

The immaculate conception is the key to the correct evaluation of grace. God could have bestowed upon Mary wealth and honor exceeding that of the greatest kings and queens. He could have made her the first lady of the world, whose favor and friendship the great ones of the world would have sought most eagerly. God did nothing of the kind for His Blessed Mother, not because He loved her less, but because He loved her more. He left her poor and insignificant in the eyes of the world, because worldly wealth and fame are like tinsel without substance and value, but "He hath clothed her with the garments of salvation, and with the robe of justice He hath covered her, as a bride adorned with jewels" (Feast of the Immaculate Conception, Introit).

If then there is any sound sense and judgment in us, let us

not waste our time and energy in running after high positions, academic honors, all the latest luxuries and comforts; all these things do not give us any intrinsic worth; they do not make us pleasing to God, but they may do grievous harm to our souls. If there is any sound ambition in us to do great things for God and souls, then our first aim must be to avoid sin in every shape and form and to strive after Christian perfection.

O Mary, conceived without sin, pray for us who have recourse to thee.


# Queen Assumed Into Heaven


MOST fittingly this title follows the preceding one, which proclaimed Mary's immaculate conception. These two titles mark the beginning and the end of her earthly life; they are the golden frame that encloses the mysteries of joy and sorrow, humiliation and exaltation which came to the Blessed Virgin as Mother of the Saviour and His companion in accomplishing the redemption of the human race. This title was inserted into the litany by decree of the Holy See of February 4, 1951.

DOCTRINE

On November 1, 1950, Pius XII, in virtue of his authority as supreme and infallible teacher of the Church, solemnly proclaimed: "Having again and again prayed to God in supplication and invoked the light of the Spirit of truth — to the honor of the almighty God who has shown a unique benevolence toward the Virgin Mary — to the honor of His Son, the immortal King of ages and Victor over sin and death — for the greater glory of the august Mother of the same Son and for the joy and exultation of the whole Church — by the authority of our Lord Jesus Christ, the blessed apostles Peter and Paul, and Our Own — We declare and define as a divinely revealed dogma that: the immaculate Mother of God and ever Virgin Mary, having completed her earthly life, was taken up into heavenly glory, body and soul."

The doctrine defined refers to the substance of the mystery of Mary's bodily assumption into heaven; it says nothing about the manner in which this was done, nor how soon after her death. Pious legends and private revelations provide some pertinent details which may be believed. It is told that by a divine inspiration all the Apostles, with the exception of Thomas, came to Jerusalem to be present at the death of the Blessed Mother of Jesus. Thomas arrived after her burial. In compliance with his ardent desire to see the earthly remains of Mary the tomb was opened. However, the tomb was empty; lilies and roses were in the place where the body had lain, a heavenly fragrance filled the tomb, and enrapturing melodies were heard coming from distant heights. It would seem highly probable that Mary was raised from the dead on the third day that she might be conformed to her divine Son.

## BASIS OF DOCTRINE

The reasons that call for Mary's bodily assumption into heaven are so strong that at no period of the Church could they have been overlooked entirely.

One of the endowments of our first parents was bodily immortality; it was lost through sin. Death entered this world as a punishment of sin; because of his proud disobedience the body of man was to return into the dust out of which it had been taken. But there was no sin in Mary. She was conceived without original sin and never did the shadow of personal sin

darken her life. Yet, where there is no guilt, there can be
no punishment. Mary died as her divine Son did, but her
body did not suffer the corruption of death. As the death of
Christ, so in a secondary way, the death of Mary was to be
the means to restore life to the world. Christ rose from the
dead, and thus as the first enjoyed the fruit of His death; must
not His Blessed Mother be the first one to do so after Him?

"The Virgin Mary is presented by the Fathers as the new
Eve, most intimately joined to the new Adam, although sub-
ordinated to Him in that struggle against the infernal enemy.
As indicated in the protoevangelium this struggle was to terminate in complete victory over sin and death. . . . Hence as the
resurrection of Christ was an essential part and crowning
trophy of this victory, so the conflict of the Blessed Virgin,
which she had in common with her Son, was also to terminate
with the glorification of her virginal body" (fourth day within
the octave of the Assumption).

Jesus loved His Mother and longed to have her with Him
in heaven, not only in soul but also in body. It is inconceivable
that He should have allowed her to become a prey of corruption. "It seems well-nigh impossible to see her, who conceived and bore Jesus, nourished Him with her milk, held
Him in her arms, and pressed Him to her bosom, after His
earthly life separated from Him in body, even though united
with Him in soul" (fourth day within the octave of the
Assumption).

Lastly, we must add, the Holy Spirit owed it to Himself
to preserve His immaculate Spouse from the corruption of the
grave. He had made her all fair, the grandest temple of the
Most Blessed Trinity — could He ever allow this temple to
fall into ruin?

## MESSAGE OF THE MYSTERY

We live in times of unprecedented materialism. On the one hand, the ambitions and efforts of the vast majority of men are centered in the gratification of material desires; on the other hand, there is found disregard for the rights of the human person, degradation and enslavement of man, contempt of human life, that does not have its equal in the past. Against this background the definition of the dogma appears in its full force of truth, encouragement, consolation, and warning. In Mary assumed into heaven we behold the dignity of man, body and soul. We too shall rise: "What is sown in corruption rises in incorruption; what is sown in dishonor rises in glory; what is sown in weakness rises in power; what is sown a natural body rises a spiritual body" (1 Cor. 15:43 ff.). Though now enslaved, tortured, starved, the faithful servant of Christ shall rise clothed in the full dignity and glory of the child of God, no longer subject to pain and death, to imprisonment and limitation of movement, to the slowness and sluggishness of matter.

Like our Mother and Queen we too shall pass through night to light, through lowliness to glory, through cross to victory, through suffering and death to immortal life. Let us not lose sight of it. "Almighty and eternal God, who didst take up into heavenly glory with body and soul the immaculate Virgin Mary, grant, we pray, that we may ever keep our minds set on the things that are above and make ourselves worthy of a share in her glory" (Collect, Feast of the Assumption).

# Queen of the Most Holy Rosary

ROSARY, in the literal sense of the word, designates a garden of roses. Most fittingly is this term applied to the well-known prayer which we call the rosary. This prayer is truly a garden, in which bloom the roses of Mary's heavenly virtues; a garden, in which we can drink from the rivers of grace and breathe in the pure and invigorating atmosphere of the supernatural. Through the rosary we not only acquire a deeper knowledge of the life of Jesus and Mary, but we are also aroused to holy love and imitation. Even a summary reflection on the mysteries of the rosary will show us how true this is.

## Joyful Mysteries

What is it that makes the mysteries of our Lord's infancy and childhood joyful mysteries? It is the fact that the Son of God became the Son of Mary; Mary is a living tabernacle, Nazareth a sacred shrine. Joy fills the home of Zachary, the Precursor is sanctified, Elizabeth is filled with the Holy Spirit at the presence of the Mother of the Lord and the first manifestation of the blessings of redemption. Heavenly peace descends upon the earth in that silent holy night at Bethlehem, in which the Saviour is born and angels sing of glory to God and peace to men of good will. It is the program of the Saviour and of all those who follow Him; to carry it out men must place themselves at the disposal of God, ready to be sacrificed. Jesus

Himself does so in His presentation and Mary presents herself for the same purpose with all the love of her heart. But often service must be rendered and sacrifice offered in the bitterness and desolation of the soul, comforted only by the consciousness that it is the will of the Father. This is the meaning of the loss of Jesus and His finding in the temple: "Did you not know that I must be about my Father's business?"

There are joyful mysteries in the Christian life unknown to the world. We are temples of the Holy Spirit, tabernacles of the Saviour after Holy Communion. He who is the light and hope of the world is within us and we can bring His blessings to our fellow men. Daily the mystery of Christmas night is re-enacted upon the altar, reminding us of our life's task: to give glory to God in order to secure the peace promised to men of good will. In baptism we were consecrated to the service of God — to be victims living, holy, pleasing unto Him; could there be a nobler joy than that of spending our life for God? And in life's lonely hours we know that God has not forsaken us, but tests our loyalty. He must be served, not because of His sweet consolation but because He is the Lord.

SORROWFUL MYSTERIES

The cross appears in many forms. All that is in man must suffer and bear the punishment of sin, either personal sin or the sins of others. The soul must suffer because mind and will are primarily responsible for sin. Therefore Jesus suffers His agony, sad unto death, trembling and sweating blood, but accepting the chalice of His Passion because it is His Father's will. The pain of the scourging atones for the sins of the flesh, all sensuality and pampering of the body; the humiliation of the crowning with thorns, for the pride by which man seeks to be like unto God and despises His will; the carrying of the cross, for the pleasure-seeking and forgetfulness of duty;

the crucifixion, for the spirit of rebellion against the restraints of God's law binding man at all times and under
all circumstances.

The sorrowful mysteries are found in the life of every
true follower of Christ. Through agony of mind and body,
through humiliations patiently borne, through fidelity in carrying the burdens of life, through perseverance in the attitude of
loving submission to God's will he must atone for sin, conform to
the image of Christ, and through such conformity with Christ
Crucified prove his claim to the glory of life everlasting.

## Glorious Mysteries

Without the glorious mysteries the work of Christ would
be incomplete and His followers would be the most miserable
among men, as St. Paul says. But Christ rose from the dead
— O death where is thy victory, O death where is thy sting?
Christ ascended into heaven to prepare a place for us — joys,
which no eye has seen, no ear has heard, no human heart
experienced. And here on earth we are not left alone in the
struggles and labors of life; Jesus has sent us the Holy Spirit,
that by the power of His love we might persevere in loyalty to
Christ unto death. A pledge and illustration of the glory to
come was given us in Mary, the Mother of Jesus. She was
raised from the dead and taken into heaven with soul and
body, and there crowned as Queen of all angels and saints,
because more than all of these she has served, suffered, and
loved unto death.

Life's struggles and sorrows will not last forever; soon they
will be over and heaven will be ours for all eternity. Thus
these glorious mysteries are a powerful call from on high to
mind the things of heaven, to view the things of this life in
heavenly light. And the power of the Holy Spirit's grace, the
intercession and help and inspiration of our heavenly Mother,

will give us peace which surpasses all understanding, joy in the midst of all tribulations. "My soul magnifies the Lord, and my spirit rejoices in God my Saviour."

May Mary, the Queen of the rosary, obtain for us an ever increasing appreciation and love of the rosary. "O God, whose only-begotten Son has by His life, death, and resurrection prepared for us the rewards of eternal salvation: grant, we beseech Thee, that recalling these mysteries by means of the most holy rosary, we may imitate what they propose and obtain what they promise" (Collect, Feast of the Most Holy Rosary).

# Queen of Peace

THIS title was added to the litany by Benedict XV during World War I. Men talked of peace and promised peace, but there was no peace, because men would not follow the ways of peace. Peace is the result of order in men's relations to God and to their fellow men. God Himself has made this order known in His commandments. When and where these commandments are ignored and transgressed there is disorder and strife. Wars, revolutions, social upheavals are the effects of the combined disorders in the moral conduct of men. Peace is meant for men of good will, but good is the will of those only who conform their will to the infinitely good will of God. According to the will of God there are some things that must be avoided and others that must be done. In both respects Mary, the Mother of the Prince of peace, leads the way and therefore she is the Queen of peace.

## DISTURBANCES OF PEACE

Any deviation from the will of God is a deviation from the way of peace, for individuals as well as nations. The first disturbance of peace occurred in heaven; it was the rebellion of the proud angels against their Creator. They would not submit to the will of God, they would not serve as He demanded. The result of this rebellion was disastrous: loss of heavenly peace and condemnation to the everlasting disorder and restlessness of hell. The second disturbance of peace took place on earth, in Paradise, and was instigated by a rebel angel. Our first parents believed the tempter more than God, and did his will rather than the will of God. The result again was disastrous: loss of grace, expulsion from Paradise, and an endless train of evils for themselves and their posterity. To the present day mankind suffers from the consequences of original sin and will do so to the end of the world.

## CONCUPISCENCE

The deadly evil bequeathed by our first parents to their posterity is concupiscence, that ever present urge to act against the order willed by God. Man rebelled against God, and in punishment his own nature now rebels against him to such an extent that St. John can say, "All that is in the world is the lust of the flesh, and the lust of the eyes, and the pride of life" (1 Jn. 2:16). This evil lust spreads its poison through seven channels, which, though different in appearance, are all alike in their deviation from the will of God; they are the so-called seven capital sins: pride, that claims equality with God and perpetuates the rebellion of the fallen angels; greed and avarice, that see an idol in the material goods of this earth; intemperance, that makes man a slave to food and drink; impurity, that lowers man even below the level of a brute; envy, that makes man sad because of the good fortune of his fellow men; anger, that does not know how to forgive and therefore seeks revenge; sloth, that sets a man craving for ease and comfort and prevents him from doing the work that would earn for him the peace of eternal life. From these vices stem all the disturbances of peace in the individual; multiplied on a national scale these vices explain the national and international disturbances of peace that plague mankind. It is in the nature of evil that it does not remain isolated in the heart, but seeks expression abroad, and thus these seven deadly streams spread their poison throughout the world.

## MARY AND THE WAYS OF PEACE

The Queen of peace possessed profound and undisturbed peace, because she was not touched by the spirit of the first rebellion on earth; she was without concupiscence, without any inordinate passion, because she was without original sin. She walked the ways of peace in perfect conformity with the will of God and practiced the virtues opposed to those seven deadly vices, amid circumstances which caused her inexpressible pain and agony of heart. She was the most humble handmaid of the Lord ever ready to do His will; she was poor in spirit without the least desire for the goods of this earth; temperate, allowing herself no food or drink beyond what was necessary to sustain her life; she was and remains the shining example of purity: the Mother most pure and chaste, the Virgin of virgins and Queen of all virgins. The Queen of peace loves men, her spiritual children, and to see them happy she allows herself to be pierced with the sword of sorrow; could she, meek and humble of heart, the Virgin merciful and Refuge of sinners, ever entertain a thought of anger or revenge? Her life is spent, her energy exhausted, in the most fervent service of God, her last breath is the last act of love in her mortal life.

These are the ways of peace; if all men followed them, national and international life would be peaceful, because there would be peace in the hearts of men. Imagine the state of the world, if there were no pride looking down upon others as inferior because of race or religion; if nations would be content with what Providence has assigned to them in territory or wealth, refrain from enslavement and exploitation of other peoples, be ready to share with others the good things which they possess in abundance; if the ideals of temperance and chastity were accepted and honored; if there were no envy of progress made by other nations, no desire for revenge; if the practice of religion were fostered in education, government, business — the result would be a truly golden age of peace.

Jesus triumphantly entering Jerusalem wept over the city and addressed to it His last warning, "If thou hadst known in this thy day, even thou, the things that are for thy peace" (Lk. 19:24). The efforts of recent popes in behalf of world peace were repetitions of this warning of the Saviour. They were not heeded and the world had to suffer unparalleled horrors of war. Let us hope and pray that, at least after these terrible experiences, men will turn to the ways of peace. The Queen of peace is eagerly waiting to lead them to her divine Son, the Prince of peace.

*Bless us, Mary, Maiden Mild.*
*Bless us, too, her tender Child!*